COACHING FOOTBALL

COACHING FOOTBALL

Larry Geigle

COACHBEAR BOOKS

CONTENTS

INTRODUCTION

Over fifty years of playing, coaching, and watching football is a pretty good reason to write down some of the thoughts on how I believe the game of football should be played. To be honest I wanted to be sure and write something down so I could remember what great fun it was to coach. My wife says I always try to live in the past, and I say why not, the past was exciting and packed full of great moments. I know you will ask yourself why would I read about what they did back in the day. Here's why those old philosophies from back in the day are gold and can help you become a better coach today. I'm sure you will find my thoughts, stories, and ideas helpful, especially if you've just started coaching, then again If you have already been coaching my book will refresh what you already know. Everything I have written down comes from hours, weeks, and years of being on the field and is firsthand information from what I remember back in the day.

CHAPTER 1

The Coach

Coachbear 30

DURING MY YEARS AS A HEAD FOOTBALL COACH, I was given the nickname Coachbear. If you happened to wander out to the football field, you could have watched the football team practicing and you couldn't help but hear or see me, Coach Geigle, yelling. I guess I sounded and looked like a big old bear in the woods. My hair would be flying in the wind as I pushed the kids toward perfection. I would be trying to set a tone for working hard in practice. If a player did something great, everybody, for half a mile, could hear my praise. If the team was dogging it, you could hear my unhappiness about that also. Even today, when I watch my grandson play, he has no problem hearing Grampa cheering him on. It was the same in baseball; I wanted their best, every day, every practice, and the *bear* wouldn't settle for any less. When computers became popular, I needed an email address, so I have always used coachbear 30 as my email. Thirty is my old high school football number, so I just tacked it onto coachbear. The kids in school, as the years went on, mostly called me Coach Geigle out of respect, but they all knew the bear at times. Even today, the bear will fire up if he needs too.

Attitude, Attitude, Attitude!

DURING MY COLLEGE DAYS, I DECIDED I WOULD PLAY FOOTBALL for the Linfield Wildcats in McMinnville, Oregon. Linfield was known for its great football teams back in the day, and today it still remains a very respected program. The only difference between today and back then and now is that Wildcats have won three national football titles and have the longest consecutive record for the number of winning season of any college in the nation. Sixty-three years without a losing season, that's not bad. Back in the day when I played, I participated and witnessed this great program being born. The coaches were and still are professional, and they do a wonderful job of showing respect and caring toward their players. At that time, my philosophy regarding playing was very simple. Do what it takes to get the job done, do it right, and do it with a smile. That's what I tried to model every day as a Wildcat. One day while I was on the field back in the day, the coach started talking with me and complimenting my hard work and great approach. He praised me for the good job I was doing and for the good football player I was becoming and how he appreciated my positive approach and willingness to work hard in practice. He went on and on. When he was done, I said thank you and told him, "It's great to be a Linfield Wildcat."

My point in telling this story is to show how the idea of doing whatever it takes to earn my coach's respect was well worth it. His praise for a job well done always lifted me up. I always remembered that conversation with my coach and applied that same approach to the football field from the day when I started coaching. I lifted my players up and gave them the confidence to get the job done. They loved to hear me call out their name and hear my voice than simply say, "GREAT JOB!" I'm retired now and I have a chance to look back at my efforts in the different jobs I performed over the years. Some jobs I admit were not my favorite. Just the same, my approach never changed. Back in the day and even now, my can-do approach to work and coaching formed a solid foundation for success in the years to come. During those years, I have received a lot of respect and benefited from doing my best and working hard. If I made a mistake, I apologized and expressed how I wouldn't try to let it happen again. In my coaching, having a positive approach always paid off, and my players played better for it. There's no question I was demanding and tough during football games and on the practice field, but every once in a while, I made sure the kids would see me smile, so they knew I loved them and I loved the game of football. To me having a positive attitude has become one of the most important ways I found to achieve success. Not giving up, working hard, doing what's right, and building a positive atmosphere of respect on and off the field are solid lessons to being a good coach.

Coach Geigle

Now that I'm retired, I look back over forty-five years of coaching, and I'm so thankful that it was a part of my life. I believe coaching was good to me because I not only loved the game, but played it for a number of years in junior high, high school, and college. I wasn't the biggest player on the field, so I hustled and played with a competitive edge. After I had played many different positions, I acquired a sound understanding and feel for the toughness and techniques needed to play the game. I tried to inspire that competitiveness in players throughout my years of coaching. My teams were hard-hitting and well prepared, along with demonstrating good sportsmanship. They were always to play within the rules of the game. I pushed my teams to believe in sustained offensive drives and aggressive in-your-face defense. I witnessed many teams who lived and died by the pass and in most cases died. Their ability to block for the running game was average, and they lost the ability to move the ball on the ground and control the clock. I've always insisted we run the football between the tackles first, play-action pass second, pass third, and offensive tricks last. I controlled the game with sustained drives, keeping the football away from our opponent then attacking them on defense.

I've watched over the years teams taking the field for their first game and can't seem to run the football. They quickly start passing and sending the wrong message, instead of insisting their lineman make their offensive blocks. Over the years of coaching offensive football, I have come to one conclusion, great teams have great offensive line coaches who developed great lineman that control the defense. It's one of the secrets to winning. Linemen are the foundation of a team's success, and finding a great line coach will help build a great team and a solid football program.

Having played the defensive line and offensive fullback positions, I realize and understand how important it is to neutralize offensive blocks and have a wrecking-ball mentality when running the football. If a defensive player wants to handle an offensive linemen's block today, he better hit the weights. For young players, doing a lot of push-ups will help build a strong upper body and for the older players, hitting the weights is essential. Upper-body strength is a must and the stronger and quicker you are the better. When taking on an offensive linemen's block, it is important to stop his initial charge then square him up while keeping him at arms' length and finding the football, releasing him, and pursuing the ballcarrier. The secret is how fast can you control and release the blocker and fly to the football and make the tackle. Coaches say it's not where you line up, it's where you end up that counts.

After years of playing fullback and then as a coach, I always looked for a running back with a wrecking-ball mentality and who were able to demonstrate good speed, blocking ability, and a real passion to find the end zone. Good fullbacks would rather take on a tackler than go around. I like that toughness and I look for a fullback that will run hard and sustain offensive blocks.

When I had finished playing in college, I put together my first football program at Highland Park Middle School in Beaverton, Oregon. I started by taking a good look at my own coaching strengths. I wanted to be sure what those strengths were so I could surround myself with assistant coaches that would complement the football program. Head coaches look for and depend on having good relationships with assistant coaches. My assistant coaches needed to be knowledgeable and positive in their coaching assignments and being part of the program.

I always felt over the years that a football program can only have one head coach who should have the final say. It's important to understand that coaching staff is a team of individuals that are working together and are respectful of each other's ideas and input. There's nothing worse than having an assistant coach who wants to do it his way or tries to coach over another coach. Coaches should express their concerns in an appropriate, respectful manner. Remember there are no shortcuts to a winning program, one head coach, one boss, one final say.

As the head coach, I tried to set the direction for the football program and help my assistant coaches and players believe in my philosophy for winning. I've always thought that a head coach needs to teach his style of offense, defense, and specialty teams that he understands and believes in. There's nothing wrong with trying something new, but new ideas need to be well thought out and used for a good reason then practiced and implemented at the appropriate time. Running a new offense or defense takes time to develop and assimilate, which can sometimes draw the coaches out of their mindset, complicating and weakening the football program.

CHAPTER 2

Coaching Football

Offensive Thoughts!

AS A COACH THROUGH THE YEARS, MY OFFENSIVE TEAMS have used the I formation. At different times we would shift into a power eye or slot backs, but our base formation was always the I. I know from experience that you need a certain amount of running and passing plays to compete in a football game. Some coaches made the mistake of having too many plays, which confuse the players and created bad timing and blocking problems. When coaching younger players, try starting with six running plays and six passing plays. Once you have decided which plays to use, push your players to run those plays with speed, timing, and sustained blocking. Remember it's critical that your linemen maintain contact with their blocks for seven counts and gain the advantage over the defense. Your running backs will need to hit the correct hole with great speed and keep their eyes up while the quarterbacks make solid handoffs. Work hard on your pass blocking to give your quarterback time to throw the football. The secret in all this is being demanding to your players, running your plays over and over to become competitive and consistent. Your players will gain confidence and consistency as the season progresses. Young quarterbacks will need to spend extra time throwing the football while getting to know their receivers and the pass routes. As the weeks go by, the number of your offensive plays should increase conservatively, but your basic offensive formations never change. Remember your basic formation is the heart of your offense and coaches, as well as the players, should be completely comfortable when using them. Over time you will realize little things that help the offensive formations work, tricks of the trade you might say—for example, flip-flopping the line or cutting down or opening up your lineman splits, going with two tight ends or putting three receivers to one side of the field. These simple adjustments have been used through the years by coaches running the same offensive plays catching the other team by surprise.

Defensive Thoughts!

Looking at defense, I have felt most comfortable running a base 5-2 defense. My belief is that the 5-2 teaches players how to read the offense, and it's what I have grown to know and use. As a defensive coach, it's good to understand all eleven defensive positions on the field and where players need to line up at any given time. Having this knowledge will draw respect from your players as well as your assistant coaches. When you want or need to go to your base defensive, just call out, "BASE DEFENSE," and all the coaches and players should know exactly what needs to happen, where to line up, and what their base defensive assignments are. Having a base defense can be a good tool for lining up and teaching new defenses and even lining up for defensive pursuit and conditioning drills.

Good Coaches

Understanding and coaching good football techniques come from many years of being a good assistant coach. I look for good assistant coaches who are not standing around talking about last week's fishing trip but are coaching. My feeling is that assistant coaches need to be coaching players talking with them and helping them get better. There's a real art to being a good assistant coach, and I always admired and respected those assistant coaches that help the program. Until you understand how to be a good assistant coach, it will be much harder to become a good head coach.

Being a coach at any level is a big responsibility. It requires many hours of discussions, drawing plays, watching and grading your team's performance, and talking with and communicating with other coaches and players. It will also include writing good practice plans, scouting opponents, and long-distance car and bus rides. As a head coach, you will learn to speak to your players before a game, inspiring and explaining to them why giving 100 percent for their team, school, parents, and community is so important and worthy of a great effort. Then at the end of the game, talk to your team once again, full of cheers and shouts of victory or the silence of being defeated. I can't tell you how many times I have been in both situations. To me football is a true classroom to teach our young people how to be strong in defeat and humble in victory while becoming great people.

The Easy and Tough Seasons

I would like to think I could have taken any group of players and had a winning season. I know the years that my teams were short on talent were the tough years. Not only did we not win games, but other parts of the football program would suffer. Coaches would start questioning what we were doing, then start looking for answers in the wrong places. Players would start wondering if they could win a football game. Parents' support would diminish, and you could feel the tension grow. I learned very quickly a football team's needs to have some talent or it's going to be a long season. It becomes a no-win situation. If the coach is pushing the players to get better and the talents are not there, then players can start having negative feelings about the program. On the other hand, if a team is winning games, the players continue to believe in their coaches and football program. I've found it's much easier for a team to get better if they're winning. I was fortunate to only have a few losing seasons in all my years of coaching different levels.

Coaching Players

Once in a while, I will witness a coach yell at a player in front of the rest of the team. I don't believe this type of coaching benefits the program or the players. It destroys confidence in players and hurts team morale. I will, however when needed, light a fire under the team's camera (butt) to practice harder! I also believe bad language on the football field by players and coaches is not acceptable. It brings down morale and takes away from being a class program. Great coaches put the player first. My reason for being on the field as a coach is to help young people grow in a positive direction in life. I will not jeopardize a student athlete's well-being to win a football game. I will, however, push my athletes to a level of performance that we as a coaching staff think they are cable of. Players need to know that coaches care about them and their well-being. I don't think I've ever met a player who wants to fail. They all have their different reason for being on the field. I've seen a first-time player playing in his first football game pick off a pass and run sixty yards down the football field to score his first touchdown. It can change his whole life. Sadly I have also seen a player crushed by what a coach said, making him feel bad about himself and taking his confidence away. I as a coach will always try to bring out the best in a player and give him an opportunity to have a great moment.

Deciding to Play

When a student or parent asked advice about playing football, I try not to force or push their decision one way or another. If it's a student, I ask a simple question, "Do you think about playing football and wonder if you might like it?" If the answer is yes, then I simply invite them to come out to practice for a few days and try the sport out. If after a few days, they aren't enjoying football, then it's okay, we thank them for trying and down the road if they change their mind they're welcome to come out try it again next season. We never make them feel bad about trying something new.

If a player already has played football or it's five weeks into the season, then our conversation is more serious. As coaches, we don't want players to look back and feel like they quit for the wrong reason and make a mistake. Parents normally like their kids to finish what they start, so we want to be sure that players, parents, and coaches are all on the same page when a player drops out. Sometimes a player will make the wrong decision and turn his gear in only to regret it later.

Some players who are overweight will find practices to be tough and want to turn in their gear. Carrying extra weight with the constant running and demands of practice can get them down. Good teams are aware of the extra effort that is needed by these players and support them in practice and cheer them on. I've seen players lose pounds by staying with it and then making huge gains in self-confidence and receiving positive reinforcement by their peers. At the end of the season, it's important to help them realize they have helped the team and gone the distance and are a better person for it.

Parents need to be careful in making the decision of whether their child can play football or not. My father almost didn't let me play football because like most parents he was afraid I would get hurt. Football literally changed my life and helped me develop as a young man. My coaches added to my life in so many positive ways. I would have hated to think about missing out on their input. I wanted to play then, and even now fifty years later, I still love the game. I still admire my coaches and see them every once in a while to say hello.

Believing in Yourself and Your Team

Have you ever wondered why coaches have winning seasons? Just like a great artist or a great singer or whatever their craft, winners love what they do and pay the price to get the job done. When I started coaching fifty years ago, I loved the game of football and wanted to become a great football coach. I realized in college I had an ability to teach others and help them achieve a higher level of performance. I then started obsessing over the different parts of a football team and how they should perform on the field. When I became a teacher in middle school, I was given my first football head coaching position. I remember talking with the football players for the first time. I had just finished coaching little league baseball and had undefeated seasons for the past two years. I wanted to do the same in football. I looked at my players sitting in the bleachers and introduced myself. I talked for a moment then took my new team outside and started running plays in a parking lot. Two weeks later we won our first two games, and then to my surprise lost the next five. I'll never forget that first year. I realized that running twenty running plays and twenty passing plays was our downfall. I decided next year to run eight running plays and eight passing plays. I was going to keep it simple. I never had another losing season. I had learned a valuable lesson to KEEP IT SIMPLE, STUPID!

If It's Working, Don't Mess with It

I remember a coach at the University Of Oregon and his last year coaching there. I watched the TV and announced to all who were watching it with me this would be this coach's last year at Oregon. They all looked at me and commented on how wrong I was; he ended up leaving the next year. When I had watched him on TV, he looked different and lacked energy standing there on the sidelines. I thought to myself, he was ready for something new and I could see that. As a head coach in the past few seasons, he had helped create a new style of football, and it changed everything. His teams were winning big. I think he loved the development process and after receiving a lot of attention for creating a winning philosophy, he wanted something bigger and started looking for a new challenge. Over the past few years, we watched him and witnessed some of his great coaching abilities. He and his coaching staff were able to create an atmosphere of great hustle and great performance. His coaching style demanded other teams defend a speeded-up style of football. Through this speeded-up offense and time management philosophy, his teams excelled to a new level. Everyone and I mean everyone watched in amazement how the Oregon Ducks performed. Coaches started changing their game plans to figure out a way to slow down the Oregon team. This new style of football started drawing some of the best athletes in the country, and they couldn't be stopped. It just got better and better. Then when he decided to leave, this new winning style of football went with him, and the big victories were over. Duck coaches tried to hold on to the ideas, but the new coaches didn't have the same vision. The football program was different now and the belief was gone.

My point is this, the head coach needs to have the confidence and the ability to put the pieces together and create a winning program. If you have a great coaching staff and your teams are winning, keep that combination of coaches together. With every coaching change, you risk changing what's working. Now that some years have passed, a new group of coaches has emerged at Oregon, with a new solid brand of football, and once again the Oregon teams are winning. Hopefully this winning combination of talent and coaches will be there for some time to come.

CHAPTER 3

Team Management

Playing away from Home

Team management on and off the field is one of the keys to having a great
football program. How your team acts in the locker room is just
as important as their performance on the field. Most teams show
great class when competing and representing their community when
playing away from home. Sadly I'm sure we've all witnessed teams
who have left the visited site after playing and earned the title of being
poorly coached. Taking a good look at how you act on the field is
worth a serious discussion. Here are some of my thoughts concerning

managing a football team on and off the field. I write about having a good attitude, doing the right thing, and being a good example for our young players. This chapter also includes thoughts about the importance of organized practices and running a disciplined team on the field while showing great sportsmanship during games.

The Huddle

A good huddle is more important than most teams give it credit for. As a coach, I watch the huddle closely to find out who's ready to play and who's not. By watching how quickly the huddle forms after a play and how well the players respond in the huddle, this shows their awareness and physical ability to compete. I will watch players for how quickly they break from the huddle and hustle to the line of scrimmage. It sends a message to the coaching staff that our team is ready to play.

We set our huddle up ten yards behind the line of scrimmage and is initiated by our center. He forms the huddle by raising his arms above his head and yelling huddle. The raising of his arms shows the players where to line up on him at that time. It is the center's job during a game to know where on the football field the football will be placed by the official for the next play. When the quarterback steps in front of the huddle, it's a signal for all players to look at him, giving him their full attention to call the play. There is absolutely no talking or distraction during the play call. When the QB calls the play, he will say it two times. After the first play call, the center and receivers will leave the huddle for the line of scrimmage to line up. The QB will call the play one more time and give the command ready break. On the break, players will clap their hands one time and yell break with the QB then hustle to the line of scrimmage. Because we flip-flop our lineman, the strong tackle and strong guard will pass in front of the weak tackle and weak guard coming out of the huddle when switching sides. When lineman approach the line of scrimmage, they will take a three-point stance looking straight ahead and not giving away who they will block. When the QB approaches, all players should be set and ready for the first sound.

Offensive Cadence

The first sound from the QB to his players at the line of scrimmage will be go. The next command will be a drawn-out ready-y-y, which gives rhythm to the cadence and helps with the timing. The QB will then yell hike and the ball will be snapped by the center to start the play. On some plays such as a QB sneak, the quarterback will approach the ball and on the first sound GO, the center will hike the football to surprise the defense. During a football game, running the football on the first sound can be used with any play and can be a real advantage done at the right time. (If you go on the first sound too often, it won't surprise the defense.) Going on the first sound is an art and needs to be practiced or it will not work.

Special Counts

Special count is an adjustment in the way a QB calls out the cadence with a hurried or sharp change in his voice catching the defense by surprise and making them jump offside. Some teams use a hard count, where the QB raises his voice on go or hike. Other teams set up the special count simply by hiking the ball on the first sound during the whole game, setting up the other team and making them think they will always go on the first sound, and then at different times during the game when yardage is needed, they surprise them by going on the second sound and making them jump offside.

Points to Remember:

1. *Your huddle needs to be sharp (no talking).*
2. *Have your players hustle to the line of scrimmage.*
3. *Repeat the play, call twice in the huddle.*
4. *QB should vary your voice when calling the play.*

5. *Always going on the first sound eliminates mistakes on offense.*
6. *Going on the first sound sets up the defense for being offside when using a special count.*

Hustling On and Off the Field

Players who are sent in or told to come out during a football game should hustle off the field. When running into a game, a player should call out the name off the player he is substituting for until the other player runs toward the sideline. Most players will high five each when going in or coming out to complete the substitution. If possible when hurt, a player should get off the field while signaling to the sidelines for a sub to play his position.

Sportsmanship on the Sidelines

During a football game, it gets pretty intense and exciting. It's easy to get too involved with the officials if you think they are making bad calls. Try to remember most officials are doing the best they can. Smart head coaches teach their players and assistant coaches to be respectful of the officials during a football game. If you yell at them too much, they might become negative toward your team. The rule for talking with officials is simple. Only the head coach is allowed to communicate with the officials. If a point needs to be made, the assistant coaches go to the head coach first, and if the head coach thinks it important enough, then he will approach the officials. If a player wants to communicate, he goes through his assistant coach. If a player is a team captain on the field, then he is allowed to approach the official in a respectful manner during a game. All players and coaches must stay back from the sidelines and must stay within the twenty-yard markers on the field during a game. Remember its okay to be excited when your team makes a great play, but inappropriate celebrating will not be tolerated by the officials and will draw a penalty. Building good relationships with the officials is to your advantage, try not to make them mad.

First Aid and Concussion Safety

It's important that the head coach and assistant coaches are certified and know the latest training on concussion protocol and first aid. As a head coach, you should also be aware of all the different drills coaches will use in practice and address any safety concerns before using them. All coaches should be trained for heat stroke and provide water breaks for the players as recommended times. A good rule is every twenty minutes providing a five-minute water break. Coaches should carry a medical file during practice and during games in case a player is injured and needs to be transported to the hospital. These medical files should also be available at all games with a list of players' phone numbers. Information should be turned into the administrative office before the transportation leaves the school. If a player is being transported by another parent, the player should submit a permission slip signed by their parent which states it's okay to be transported. The parent transporting the player should also turn in proof of insurance and a valid driver's license to the school's administrative office before transporting a player. Players should not be allowed to wear sports equipment that has not been certified for safety by the school district or youth football organization.

Coach Sets the Pace

Last summer, I was sitting in the bleachers at Mountainside High School in Beaverton, Oregon, watching the new football coach run his players through their practice. I was there to support my grandson, Landon Sherman, in his attempt to make the varsity team. I had watched Landon through the years, starting out when he was just a little guy. From the moment he started playing, he loved the game of football and enjoyed competing and being part of a team.

Sitting there, I watched as the new coach pushed his players to work hard—putting pressure on them, breaking from the huddle, running up to the line of scrimmage, then quickly hiking the football. He was teaching his players that doing things at a faster tempo creates a winning edge, helps with conditioning, and presents an atmosphere of hustle. As I continued to watch, it was pretty evident that you did what the coach wanted and earned the right to play or you rode the bench. There were no free rides on this team; everyone pulled their weight. I also saw that if a player made an honest mistake, he was immediately surrounded by the other players, who made sure he felt a wave of positive support, letting him know to shake it off.

I leaned back on the bench with the warm rays of the sun hitting my face and admired the attention to detail in drills and watched the coach's ability to run the show. I knew very quickly he was a seasoned educator and was born to coach. His assistant coaches gave him the respect he deserved and listened to his every word, knowing that his many years of experience were earned. As the head coach, he was here to lead these young athletes and their new high school to victory. We all felt he was the right choice and a great addition to Mountainside High School. He had brought his wisdom of football from years of experience, winning and losing. His philosophy was ingrained into all his high school teams from lessons learned by performing hundreds of hours of practice, meetings, watching a film, and playing games on Friday nights. I was very pleased that my grandson was having this man in his young life.

Being a retired coach myself, I knew this coach knew the secrets of winning, having won the high school state title at Silverton High school in Silverton Oregon before coming to Mountainside.

While sitting there, I had plenty of time watching practice and thinking back about my days as a coach and teacher and how over the years I had gained wisdom and experience in coaching. I then focused on the field looking down at the coach. I watched this seasoned leader and smiled. This guy had my respect. He had earned the right of passage and earned the right to make the important football decisions. This leader had been in hundreds of situations and drew from his experiences knowing what to do, what works, and what doesn't.

It's pretty easy for me, as a retired coach, sitting there on those hard-metal bleachers to appreciate the wisdom being used down on the field. I started thinking about the world today and how we're trying to pass that wisdom on to a future generation. It seems in this fast-paced world, many people want to lead without having learned the tough lessons that time can teach us. I've seen and met many who call themselves leaders after finding an early entry into a leadership role and wanting just to make their mark and achieve recognition. I've witnessed these leaders and their lack of ability to handle people and serious situations. They have a suitcase full of new ideas that haven't been thought out but sounded good, then using their voice, telling people what they want to hear while looking for instant creditability, attention, and fame. These unseasoned leaders push their way into leadership and truly believe they have arrived then quickly get in over their heads and find out they don't have wisdom or experience to draw from. The impact of these types of leaders over time can keep us from doing things right then clouding our vision, making us forget how we got here in the first place. Smart leaders, who have seen change, welcome new ideas but have also seen many ideas come and go. They realize that making a change can be both rewarding and costly at the same time. Seasoned leaders know too many changes too quickly can lead to loss of direction and confusion and bring about a negative result. Wisdom tells us we need to use common sense and pay attention to our leaders.

<u>Change comes from good decisions over time to achieve good results.</u>

Taking one last look from high in the bleachers, I look down at the field; practice is now coming to an end, and it's been a good day. Down on the field, the team is starting to look pretty good and we all know why. Our head coach is a great leader, and it seems wherever he goes the sun shines brightly. His football program has evolved over the years without too many changes to a football philosophy that has served him well. My grandson's in good hands! Go, MAVERICKS!

Post Script

The football season is over now and the Mountainside Mavericks with eight wins and four losses made it to the playoffs. Not only did they make it to the playoffs, but they knocked off the number-one-rated team in the state the Tigard Tigers, 34-31, in an exciting overtime finish that will go down in Oregon High School history. Never has a number-sixteen-rated team knocked off a number-one-rated team in the history of Oregon High School football. As of this moment, they have not won the state title, but there is always next year. Landon Sherman #12 made the third team, all Metro, and is looking forward to his next season as a Maverick with our coach at the helm. As a grandfather, I sit here very proud of my grandson and the team for going the distance and Coach and his staff for the fine job this year!
Coach Geigle Fall of 2019

Practice and Repetition

Practice and repetition are two of the true secrets to becoming truly good at your craft. Through many hours of practice, you become aware and sensitive to the small important details that set you apart from others. You learn to feel, smell, touch, hear, and see the secrets to becoming better. During hundreds of hours of practice and repetitions, you will experience many victories and some defeats. Celebrate the victories and hold them close, they will give you the confidence to move forward. Learn from the defeats and remember what you learned. Don't dwell on the losses, let it pass, and don't look back; continue your journey. Remember defeats are part of the process of greatness. At times you might need to step back and take a break. reflecting on where you've been and where you're headed. Even then during your break without knowing it, you will still be growing and processing the secrets you have learned. The truly good artists (coaches) come from seasoned veterans who over years have acquired wisdom and skill through practice, repetition, and most of all time.

Practice Tempo and Accountability

Practice and repetition are lost without accountability and tempo. Your team's improvement depends on what type of atmosphere you develop in practice. Football is a sport played with a time-sensitive and competitive environment. Going through practice at a slow, noncompetitive pace and not insisting that your players perform is the road toward average at best. Performing at an upbeat-practice tempo sets the stage for your players to be in better physical shape, catch more footballs, block better, run plays harder, and make more tackles. This list goes on and on. If your team isn't working hard in practice, then it's your job as a coach to light a fire under their butt and give them a reason to try harder. It's more important that the player respect coaches first and like them second. Practice tempo is one of the secrets to success on the football field. Lazy talent is inconsistent and will lead to an average play and a lack of success under pressure.

Practice Schedules

When I was hired for my first head football coaching position, my first obligation to the athletic director was turning in a daily practice plan. He was not only the athletic director but also my offensive line coach. It turned out to be one of the most important obligations of my formative years in coaching. Every day I would sit and write down what I thought should happen in football practice and laid out a minute-by-minute schedule. Through this process, I had a record of what we had accomplished in the previous practices, what was needed in future practices, and what did or did not work. I could also evaluate the time used for offense, defense, and special teams.

As the season progresses, writing practice schedules got easier and on most days really didn't take that long. I was always sure to print off copies, and I made sure the other coaches got a practice schedule in time to read it before practice. After practice, while the players were dressing and heading home for the day, the other coaches and I would meet and talk about practice for the next day and concerns and give positive feedback about the recent practice. The point I'm making is this, the head coaches should write practice plans as a daily routine. Your assistant coaches need to have a practice plan in their hands so they know how much time they have and what the practice is going to look like. Then they can get ready and adjust their coaching time to run drills. The following is a sample of a daily practice plan.

Football Practice Plan (Example)

Monday 2, 2000

<u>Before-practice warm-up</u>

3:30 p.m.–3:45 p.m.—specialties—center snaps, punting, punt return, center long snaps, kickoffs, kickoff returns.

QB and receiver passing warm-up—patterns, hook, slant, post, flag, go.

<u>Practice starts</u>

3:45 p.m.–4:10 p.m. warm-ups—six lines—<u>team captains out front facing the six lines,</u> players five yards apart, five yards deep.

<u>Exercises</u>

jumping jacks, stretches, crunches, squats, push-ups, karaoke, backward run, high knee skip, frontward and backward, shuffle down and back, twenty-yard sprint down and back two times.

4:10 p.m.– 4:30 p.m.—individual defense
Defensive backs—Coach Sherman
tackling drill, straight on, angle
stance, starts
defensive ball drill
read run or pass drill
cover 1–cover 2–cover 3

Linebackers—Coach Oliver
tackling drill, straight on, angle
stance, starts
shuck drill
defensive run-and-pass drill

Defensive Line—Coach Geigle
tacking drill, straight on, angle
stance starts
read drill
shuck drill
pass-rush drill

4:30 p.m.–4:35 p.m. water break

4:35 p.m.–5:05 p.m. team defense
Team-Pursuit Drill
Base 5-2 cover 1, 2, 3
Base 5-2 linebacker stunts
Base 5-2 tackle loop
Pass containment lanes
Team defense vs. scout team
Punt return
Kickoff return

Offense
5:05 p.m.–5:25 p.m. offensive specialty

<u>Line</u>
<u>Coach Sherman</u>
stance, starts, first step
pull right and left, pass
sled or dummies, getting off the ball, seven-count block
man block, down block, double-team block, trap block, pass block
offensive plays --- review run-and-pass offense --- intro new plays

<u>Running Backs</u>— Coach Geigle
Hand offs, sweep, pitch, ball grip (protect the ball)
pass and run blocking, swing pass
offensive plays—review run-and-pass offense, intro new plays

<u>Offensive Receivers</u>—Coach Oliver
stance starts, catching the ball
review pass routes—slant, hook, out
post, seam. flag
plays—review run-and-pass offense, intro new plays

<u>5:25 p.m.–5:30 p.m. water break</u>

<u>5:30 p.m.–5:55 p.m. team offense</u>
1. practice run-and-pass offense against scout team
2. good play call, good huddle, good approach to the ball
3. get off the ball, get a push, hitting the holes
4. good blocks, good team spirit, and hustle
5. good pass routes, good pass protection
6. punt team—3 seconds to punt the ball
7. kickoff—long, line drive, on side

<u>5:55 p.m.—open—conditioning</u>
Run sprints—40 yards, 30 yards, 20 yards, 10 yards
6:00 p.m.—locker room

Senior Leadership Varsity Football

Every year you can hear the start of high school football programs once again hitting the field. The sounds of jumping jacks, team cheers, and coaches expressing themselves in a variety of voices pushing our kids to be the best they can be.

With every new year brings awareness to a new group of seniors who are asked to mentor the underclassmen. Their job is to pass on the torch for a winning season and provide toughness, perfection, brotherhood, and respect for all players who are on the team.

As a head coach of a winning program, it's important that the seniors are given the responsibility of setting a tone for the rest of the players. At the end of the first practice, seniors will call the team together and talk about what's expected and the effort needed to achieve success. I believe this is a big part of the educational process of being part of a high school football team. Seniors need to walk their talk and set the example in handling everyday activities in school and on the football field concerning behavior, language, locker-room atmosphere, classes, attendance, effort, and most of all winning and losing. Seniors watch over the team and make sure football is positive for younger players, the school, and the community.

Captains are chosen at the start or end of a football season, according to individual programs. I've found that giving the responsibility to all the seniors is more powerful than choosing one or two to run the show the entire season. With each new week during the season, different seniors are chosen for the upcoming game. Picking new captains every week gives the opportunity to all seniors to lead and keep the spirit of the team alive! Week after week, the seniors will make sure practices go well, and everyone works hard getting ready to win the next game. Then on Friday night, win or lose, seniors captains help set the tone to lead by example when winning or losing. When the team is victorious, it's the captain's job to teach younger players to be humble and thankful about their victory showing respect for the team they have just beaten. If it was a loss, then hold their heads up and show good sportsmanship and respect to the winning team.

Do the Right Thing

This story is about stealing or the theft of someone else's property. I remember back when I was in my early days as a teacher. I was barely making ends meet, and I would get up at four in the morning and deliver five hundred *The Oregonian* newspapers by car every morning seven days a week to make ends meet supporting my wife and new baby girl. After delivering the newspapers, I would race home, take a hot shower, and then go on to school and teach a full day of classes.

One morning I was driving along delivering papers and came upon a beautiful little statue sitting along the side of the road just a few feet up a dirt bank. I stopped my car and sat there looking at the statue for a minute or two, then got out, walked over, climbed up the bank and picked up the statue, and then returned to my car and set the statue in the back seat. While I was picking it up, I was thinking about how wonderful it would look on the front porch of the new little house we had just bought. I quickly drove off and continued to deliver my papers. As I drove, negative thoughts immediately started invading my head. Even though the statue was sitting on the side of the road and it appeared to be abandoned, my mind started telling me it wasn't mine, and I had actually taken someone else's property. I drove on for a while until my thoughts were beating me up so badly I swung the car around and headed back to where I had found the statue. When arriving, I stopped the car grabbed the statue from the back of the car and quickly placed it back where I had found it, got in, and drove off.

Immediately I was relieved and my thoughts drifted as to what had just happened. I started thinking about how I would have gone home taking the statue and placing it on our front porch. Then every day when coming home from work, I would have walked up to our front walk and approached it. Every day it would have been sitting there staring at me and reminding me how it wasn't mine and it was stolen property. Of course my wife would have asked where the statue came from, and I would have to make up a story and start lying to her or telling her the truth about how I had taken it from the side of the road. She would have been upset and the statue would have never been something we could have enjoyed because it wasn't really ours; it had a black cloud hanging over it.

As a coach throughout the years, I would tell this story to my players to get them thinking about not taking property that belonged to their teammates in the locker room. I wanted them to clarify their own thoughts about theft and think about how it would bring the team down. How would they feel if something would be stolen from them? Lastly I would talk about being smart pertecting and developing good habits to keep one's personal property safe. I always ended the story with encouragement to do the right thing.

A Boy Named Joe: Why I Coached Football

This is about a boy named Joe. Joe came from a family with four, very large sons. Joe's dad was six foot seven inches and a mountain of a man. Joe's brothers Pete, Stan, and Willie were just like their father—big, strong, and fast. All three boys played college and then pro football. When Joe became one of my students in the ninth grade, he wanted to be like his big brothers and play football. Joe had a learning disability but made up for it with his sense of humor and enthusiasm.

During the school year, Joe helped me with a fundraiser by putting on a haunted house. We set up a fake operation in the boys' PE dressing room in the teachers' office. Joe played a doctor operating on someone who was lying on an operating table under blue lights. He used hamburger as bloody guts and had also made a recording of a heartbeat that lasted an hour, using his own voice for the sound effects. He played the heartbeat as people walked by and looked through the window, watching him operate. Then he would slowly turn and look at them and walk toward the door to open it as if to grab one of them like a mad scientist. It looked like the real thing. The haunted house made over two thousand dollars that night, and Joe was the big hit.

Joe's learning handicap prompted a tough discussion on whether it was safe for him to play football. As the head football coach, I could see the sadness that Joe was feeling by being told he couldn't play. At that time, we had two ninth-grade football teams. One team was made up of bigger players and the other team was smaller players. We did this to make the games safer and more competitive. After getting to know Joe, even though he was a tall kid with his disability, he would fit right in with the smaller team. Getting permission for him to play was not easy. Explaining to the staff why Joe should have a chance to be like his brothers wasn't easy.

When I finally had convinced the staff to allow Joe to try out for the team and was able to tell him; his eyes lit up and he walked around the school proud that he was going to be a football player. When practice started, I kept a close eye on Joe and made sure he was practicing with players close to his ability. The first time Joe was knocked down in a blocking drill, he started to cry. He just lay there on the ground weeping. I told all the players to move ten yards downfield and continued the drill. I told Joe when he was done crying that the team would be downfield and get up and get back in line. I also told him, "Welcome to football." After a while, I watched as he got to his feet and got back in line for the drill. When it was his turn again, he got knocked down. Again he started to cry again, so I moved the team, this time not saying a word. I was letting Joe decide whether he was going to play football or not. Joe got up and got back in line and was ready, once again, for his turn. This time, I told Joe that he needed to knock the whoop-tee-do out of the other player. You could see the determination in Joe's eyes. When the ball was hiked and the two players came together, Joe drove his opponent down the field, ten yards. The other players went crazy, cheering Joe on then surrounding him, patting him on the back, and telling him what a great job he had done. Joe was smiling from ear to ear. He never cried again. Joe went on to be the starting right tackle for the lightweight team and had a wonderful season. Joe was voted the most inspirational player by his teammates. He never played football again after that year, but we all knew it had changed him forever. Joe's family thanked me for all I had done. In the spring Joe became my baseball equipment manager and did a tremendous job, always wearing a big smile. I loved that guy!

CHAPTER 4

Offense

Putting the Offense Together

When starting to put an offensive team together, the coaching staff should be looking at their players' abilities. Coaches should meet and determine what will be their offensive strong points. I, myself, as the head coach start looking for players I think will be important to win football games. I then share my thoughts with the other coaches. By the end of our preseason meetings, we should have a pretty good idea who our players are and what position they're going to play. Because we know our first practice is a starting point, we always want to be fair and be ready for someone to surprise us with their growth during the past year. During the offseason, I try to have many conversations with different players, talking with them about changes in their abilities concerning strength, speed, quickness, and all-around performance. I keep a close eye on what they're doing in school concerning their grades and citizenship. Here's what we're looking for in the different offensive positons to be a successful offensive team.

Tight Ends

Tight ends need to be tall and strong. They must be able to block big defensive linemen and linebackers as well as run good pass patterns and have the ability to catch the football. We want that tough durable quality. I also believe the tight end needs to be very good at deceiving defensive players on pass routes. He's going to change his stance with each new play called. When drive blocking his man downfield, his outside foot will be staggered slightly back to get a better push off the line. When blocking down on the tackle, he is going to even up his stance in order to slant down. On a pass play, he will need to widen his split to get a cleaner release. Lastly when it's a running play to the outside, he will reduce his split so the running back can turn the corner quicker.

Strongside Tackle

Our strongside-offensive tackles are our biggest and strongest offensive players. Here's what we look for. These players are not quite as fast but can still get down the field even though they're big, tall, and strong. Our strong tackles become the foundation of our offensive line and make important line calls. They are determined to defeat their opponent. They must have the ability to protect the quarterback on pass plays and drive the opponent downfield on the running plays. The strongside tackle stance needs to be a balanced three-point stance with a staggered outside foot back. He should be able to get a good push off the line of scrimmage on running plays and is able to set up quickly for pass blocking.

Strongside Guard

The strongside guards must be able to get off the ball quickly to block linebackers and pull on the counterplay. They are strong and able to block big defensive lineman. The strongside guard should be a good pass blocker and able to pick up stunts and seal off the inside containment lanes. I look for them to be aggressive, consistent, and determined to defeat their opponent. They have the same three-point stance as the weakside guard. Their outside foot needs to be staggered back slightly, allowing them to set up quickly to protect the quarterback on pass plays and get off the ball on running plays.

Center

Centers are smart and most of all consistent. They must center the ball time after time without a mistake. The center must be able to hike the ball and fast enough to get downfield to block a linebacker. He shows leadership, consistency, and draws respect from the other players. It would be great if the center had some height but not mandatory. The center must also work with the other lineman and be a good pass-rush blocker.

Weakside Guard

Weakside guards are smaller and faster than the strongside guard. They must be fast enough to block down on the nose guard and the backside linebacker on running plays. We name our weakside guards not because he's weak but because we realize in most schools there are only so many big linemen. Our weakside linemen are just a little smaller and quicker, but make no mistake they are expected to control the defensive blocker and set up quickly to protect the quarterback. The weakside guard stance changes with the play called. If he's blocking straight ahead, then he will stagger his outside foot slightly back to get a better push off the line. If he is going to pull, then we would like him to even up his stance not to give away which way he's pulling.

Weakside Tackle

When looking for a weakside tackle, I know he will be quicker and not quite as strong as our strongside tackle. He will be asked to shut down the outside containment lane on a pass rush and also get down the field to help block on the running plays. Once again like all our linemen, they are the key to our success moving the football. The weakside tackle will be a hard worker and loves to compete. His stance is a three-point stance with the outside foot staggered back to get a push downfield to cut off a deep backside defender.

Getting Ready to Play (Talking with the Line)

Before a game, I will find a place where I can talk with the linemen. I want to make sure they understand what our goals are when we take the field. The first point I try to make is how important their success on the field is to us winning a football game. They need to be relentless in staying with their blocks on both running and passing plays. I then talk about maintaining their blocks for at least seven seconds even though I know as a coach that five seconds would be great. I express to the linemen that their greatest moment blocking their opponent is gaining the advantage and putting him on his back. As I continue my conversation, I talk about getting off the ball together like a fine-tuned machine play after play, holding their blocks. I tell them I don't want our quarterback touched on pass plays, and they need to be determined about protecting him. Last I express the importance of no penalties, such as holding and blocking in the back and offside. As we get ready to join the rest of the team, I once again express the importance of beating the man across from them. My last comment is for our team to use good sportsmanship and leave all they have to give on the field.

Split Ends

Split ends must be able to catch the football first, run second, and then be able to block downfield. They must have speed and the ability to fake out the defender. Making key catches in a football game is crucial. Having great hands, spending extra hours catching the football on timing routes, and keeping their feet in bounds are all important qualities needed to win. Split ends are normally tall and can go up in the air to make a catch. We ask our split ends to have an upright stance with one foot staggered behind the other. We want their hands hung down to their side looking at the defense and at the same time be aware of the football being snapped. Our split ends will drive hard off the ball when it's snapped for the defensive backs outside leg to makes their moves.

Tailback

The tailback should be our most talented ballcarrier. He will have the speed to go outside and the toughness to carry the football inside. The tailback needs to able to block at times and pass the football. He also becomes a receiver on certain plays. When the tailback is aligned behind the fullback, he is in an upright stance with his hands on his thighs with the fingers pointed in and slightly down. He should be one or two yards deep behind the fullback in order to find the best opening on the running play. We ask the tailback to open step in the direction he's going. His first step helps set up his blocks and gives him a slight advantage over the defender to adjust. He is very hard to tackle and has a natural gift to carry the football.

Fullback

Our fullbacks are big and strong and like to carry the ball up the middle. They would rather run over the tackler instead of going around him. They are good at keeping their feet moving and hanging on to the football. Great fullbacks will destroy linebackers and defensive ends with their blocks and are able to catch the football. The fullback must be able to lead block for the tailback on inside plays and outside running plays. They are able to pick up yards in short-yardage situations. We also like him to carry the ball on the option play inside if we run it. The fullback must be an excellent actor when faking handoffs. His stance is a balanced three-point so he can go right or left when the ball is hiked. He should lead step in the direction toward the hole he is going to. He should be smart enough to vary his depth on different plays. If he is going to block the defensive end *inside out,* he should line up *shallower,* and if he is going to block the end *outside in,* then line up *deeper.* This will help with his blocking angles when setting up his blocks. He must be crafty not to give the play away by where he lines up.

Slotback

The slotback is not as big as our other backs, but he is fast and a good runner as well as a good receiver. He must be able to help block on the inside running plays. The slotback stance is upright with his feet balanced, able to go right and left quickly. His hands are on his thighs with fingers pointed down. He lines up off the ball one yard deep and one yard outside the hip of the weak tackle. When asked to go in motion, he moves quickly to help confuse the defense. We see him as being quick and elusive.

Quarterback

When looking for a quarterback, a number of qualities are needed. We would like our quarterback to be a ball handler first, a passer second, and a runner third. He possesses leadership, desire, and the ability to move the team down the field. He is smart, poised, and plays at a high level in games and is admired by his teammates. Our quarterback stance is feet parallel and hunched over behind the center. This enables the quarterback to move right or left quickly and gives room for the guard to pull. The QB needs to show us a good exchange between him and the center. We look for him to place his thumbs together then rotate his hands to the left until the middle finger of the right-hand splits the butt of the center. His thumbs should always touch. His elbows are slightly flexed to allow for the center's first movement. When the QB receives the ball, he should quickly pull the ball to his stomach as he pivots and moves along the line. We want him to use an open or reverse pivot step, always keeping weight on the planted foot. On the handoff to the ballcarrier, the QB places the football in the back's stomach. The back receives the ball with his inside elbow raised up and to the QB and his outside elbow down and out. When the QB places the ball, the back brings his arms and hands over the ball to secure it. On pitch-out plays, our QB will reverse pivots and pitch the ball firmly to the running back using both hands. He aims for the back's waist, leading him slightly. When passing the football, there are some key points to remember. On sprint-out passes, our QB should be able to square his shoulders to the line of scrimmage when delivering the football. The ball should be thrown chest high with very little lead time because the receiver is also moving. The ball should always be thrown away from the defender so he will have trouble getting to the ball and knocking it down or intercepting it. When throwing passes downfield, the QB needs to show he can throw the ball with a lot of air so the receiver can run to it. Once again throwing the ball to an area away from the defender. When a right-handed QB shows, rolls out to his left, and throws to his backside, he should be getting enough depth so he can square his shoulders to the line of scrimmage and throw off his left foot.

Line Blocking Techniques

I feel it is important to know some basic line blocks used in the running game and passing game before talking about our basic offensive plays.

Drive Block (Man-on-Man)

The first block we teach our linemen is the drive block. It's just like it sounds. The linemen will get in his three-point stance when the ball is hiked; he will step with his inside foot staying low and shooting his hands toward the defensive player's chest, driving up and through the man. Once contact has been made the offensive linemen will try and turn the defensive man away from the running lane being attacked. It is important that during the block, the lineman uses short, wide choppy steps and gets his camera (butt) toward the ballcarrier. All offensive blocks last seven seconds or seven counts. The secret to having a good line is to insist that your linemen keep contact with the defensive player for seven counts. Some teams don't insist on the seven counts and come off their blocks too early. Seven counts no less, that's the secret!

Double-Team Block

The next block is a double-team block; again it is just like it sounds. The double-team block starts with the offensive linemen who is ahead up over the defensive player standing him up and driving him back. The offensive lineman who is to his right blocks down and drives into the defensive player with his near shoulder. Both offensive linemen work hard as a team to move the defensive player away from the hole.

Trap Block (Pulling)

Our pull block is used on trap plays or sweeps. Again it is exactly like it sounds. The offensive lineman pulling right or left will turn and open step with the foot closest to the direction he is going. It's important that he doesn't step backward or lose ground. He should travel straight down the line, blocking the defensive player inside out away from the running lane. If he does give ground, it will crowd the offensive QB and running backs handoff exchange. Pull blocks are performed with speed and deception by trying to surprise the defensive player and take advantage of the blocking angle.

Pass Block

Pass blocking is done to protect the quarterback when trying to pass the ball downfield. When pass blocking, your stance should be balanced and look the same as the run. In the past you could tell a lineman was going to pass block by the way he set up in his stance. They would also give the runaway by too much of their body weight leaning forward. Now you must try to look the same run or pass. When pass blocking, your first step is back with your inside foot and then your outside foot keeping a wide base, knees bent, and your hands up ready to contact the defender's charge. Once contact is made, you try and ride your defender to the outside or in a direction away from the quarterback. Maintaining contact with the defensive player is important to protect the QB. Remember seven-count block!

Formations

I have always used a strongside and weakside offensive line. The players will flip-flop from side to side depending on the line call. I will flip-flop my line to place my strong players over the opponent's weaker or lazy players to gain the advantage. I try to keep it simple and only use two words to flip-flop the players. When we call I right, the tight end, strongside tackle, and the strongside guard line up to the right of the center. When we call I left, it's just the opposite, the tight end, strongside tackle, and the strongside guard will line up to the left of the center. The first word is the formation call; the second word is the placing of our strongside players. The weakside guard and tackle always flip-flop together and the strongside guard, strongside tackle, and tight end always go together. The split end will always go to the weakside and splits out ten to fifteen yards. The slotback also goes to the weakside and aligns himself one yard deep and one yard outside the weak tackle. Our fullback lines up behind the center three yards deep. The tailback sets up two yards behind the fullback or five yards from the line of scrimmage. This is our basic I formation and the start of our offensive package.

The next thing we would call in the huddle would be a number telling us which back is going to get the ball through which hole on the line of scrimmage. For example, I right 32 dive, this means we're in an I formation, our strongside guard, strongside tackle, and tight end are to the right and we're going to hand the football to the three back (fullback) through the two holes on the line of scrimmage and our tailback will fake a sweep right.

Our offensive backs are number in this manner. Our QB is number one, tailback number two, our fullback number three, and our slotback number four. Our holes on the line of scrimmage go odd to the left 1, 3, 5, 7. Our center is zero. Then even to the right 2, 4, 6, 8. The gaps between the linemen are one and a half feet. The tight end is two and a half yards outside the strong tackle on run and three yards on passing plays. You should now have a good idea of how we line up on the ball. The next few pages will explain our basic blocking rule and show our numbering system.

Basic Blocking Rule

We use a basic blocking rule for our offensive linemen when confused about who they block. When this happens, they can refer to a basic blocking rule. The rule is easy to remember and can be used quickly. It goes like this, INSIDE, ON, OVER, AND OUTSIDE. If you're an offensive lineman and want to use your basic blocking rule, first check your *inside* gap to the play side or the side the football is being run. If no one is on your inside gap, then you would check *on* to see if a defensive player lines up in front of you. If the answer is no, then you would check *over* which means a defensive player has lined up over you but back a few yards like a linebacker. If there's no one over you then you would check your *outside* gap. Once again the basic blocking rule is *inside, on, over, and outside.* Have your players say it over and over so if they're ever confused about their blocking assignment, they can use the basic blocking rule to help them.

When our lineman block for a running play we, coaches, teach them to always end up with their camera (butt) to the ballcarrier. We want them between the defensive man and the ballcarrier as the play develops. This is a very important coaching point and needs to be practiced daily. We also tell our lineman to get upfield and block a second man if they can. If they're completely out of the play, then it's important they don't draw a penalty by a block in the back (clipping) or holding. We work really hard at trying to keep penalties in a football game to a minimum.

Basic Offensive Formations and hole numbering

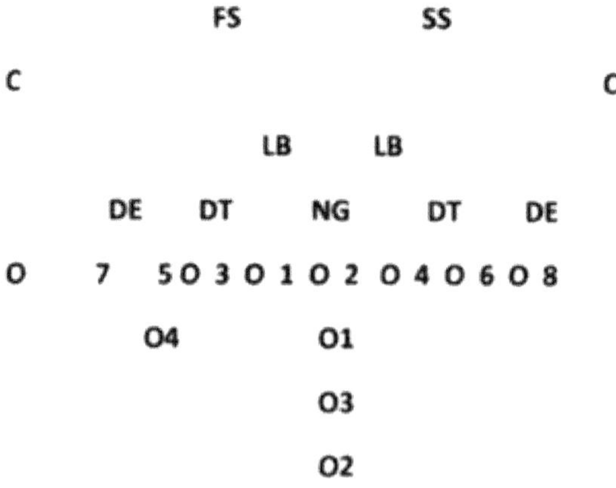

CHAPTER 5

Run Offense

Quarterback Sneak

The quarterback sneak is used when you need a very small amount of yardage, or you just want to surprise the other team because their defense is slow to line up. When running the QB sneak, the quarterback will be the last player to come up to the line of scrimmage after the play is called in the huddle. All lineman should be lined up and set when he approaches the center. They will decide who to block using their basic blocking rule inside, on, over, and outside). The center will hike the ball on the quarterbacks first sound.

Responsibilities

Tight End
The tight end blocks the defensive end inside out seven counts or until the whistle is blown.

Lineman
The Lineman blocks inside out using their basic blocking rule. They block seven counts or until the whistle is blown.

Slotback
The slotback seal blocks for seven counts or until the whistle is blown.

Split End
The tight end will seal block the cornerback from the ballcarrier, seven-count block or until the whistle is blown.

Fullback and Tailback
Fullback blocks right and the tailback fakes sweep action right.

Quarterback
QB runs the football on the first sound through the 1 or 2 hole.

Points to Remember:

1. *Be ready when QB approaches the line of scrimmage.*
2. *Don't give the play away.*
3. *Run the QB sneak when the defensive team is lazy or slow lining up.*
4. *Hold onto the football no fumbles.*

Quaterback Sneak

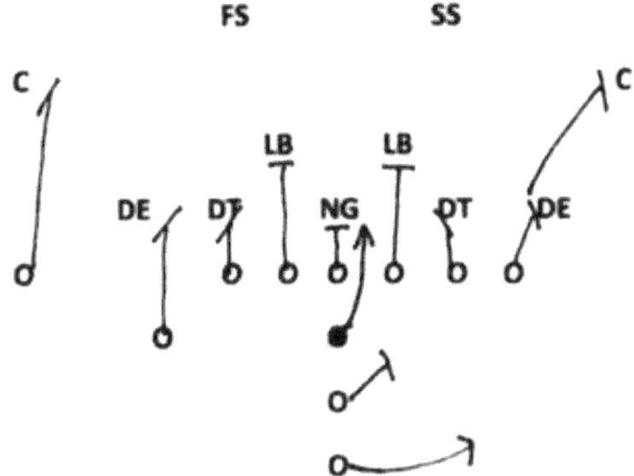

The 31 and 32 Fullback Dive

The fullback dive is a play I've used over the years for some tough yards. I look for the linebackers to play far off the line of scrimmage. If they do, I run a quick dive to our fullback on the quarterback's first sound to gain the advantage and pick up the short yardage. It keeps me from beating up my quarterback with quarterback sneaks. The fullback hits the 1 or 2 hole fast and hard. The quarterback barely has time to hand the football off. If needed, I can also call a fullback 34 or 35 dive depending on the defensive alignment, but in most situations, it's the 31 and 32 dive because it hits the line of scrimmage so quickly. The lineman uses a straight-man block using their basic blocking rule (inside on, over, and outside) which keeps the play very simple and quick. Once again we ask for a seven-count block or until the whistle is blown. The lineman turns their camera (butt) to the ballcarrier as the play develops. The tailback fakes a sweeping motion to the play side.

Responsibilities

Tight End

The tight end has a seal block on the defensive end. His block is seven counts or until the whistle blows. He turns his camera (butt) to the ballcarrier as the play develops.

Strongside Tackle

The strongside tackle, in most cases, seal blocks the defensive tackle to his outside, sealing him off from the ballcarrier. He uses his basic blocking rule (inside, on, over, and outside) to determine who to block. Once again it's a seven-count block or until the whistle is blown. He wants to turn his camera (butt) to the ballcarrier as the play develops.

Strongside Guard

The strongside guard drive blocks the play-side linebacker out of the dive hole seven counts or until the whistle is blown. If possible, we would like the strong guard to block his man from the inside freeing up the running lane to the outside.

Center

The center refers to his basic blocking rule (inside, on, over, and outside) and seal blocks his man to the inside away from the ballcarrier. Like always, he blocks for seven counts or until the whistle is blown. He wants to turn his camera (butt) to the ballcarrier as the play develops.

Weakside Guard

The weakside guard seal blocks the backside linebacker seven counts or until the whistle is blown. He turns his camera (butt) to the ballcarrier as the play develops. He uses his basic blocking rule (inside, on, over, and outside) to determine who to block.

Weakside Tackle

The weakside tackle check blocks the backside defensive tackle from the ballcarrier. He then goes after the free safely. He blocks seven counts or until the whistle is blown. His camera (butt) should be turned to the ballcarrier. The basic blocking rule is used (inside, on, over, and outside) to determine who to block.

Slotback

The slotback seal blocks the backside defensive end or outside linebacker from the ballcarrier. His block is seven counts or until the whistle is blown. He turns his camera (butt) to the hole as the play develops. He refers to his basic blocking rule (inside, on, over, and outside).

Split End

The split end stalk blocks the cornerback from the ballcarrier. His blocks are seven-count or until the whistle is blown. He turns his camera (butt) to the ballcarrier.

Fullback

Fullback open steps for the 2 hole and receives the handoff from the quarterback. He runs off the inside hip of the strong guard through the 2 hole for as many yards as he can look to cut outside.

Quarterback

The quarterback's number one job is to get the football to the fullback. He turns to his right and hands the football off to the fullback and fakes sweep action down the line with the tailback.

Tailback

Tailback opens steps to his right and fakes sweep to the play side.

Points to Remember:

1. *QB makes a clean handoff.*
2. *This is a quick hit fullback dive.*
3. *Stay with your block seven counts.*
4. *Fullback hangs on to the football.*
5. *Good fake by the QB and tailback.*

I Right 32 dive

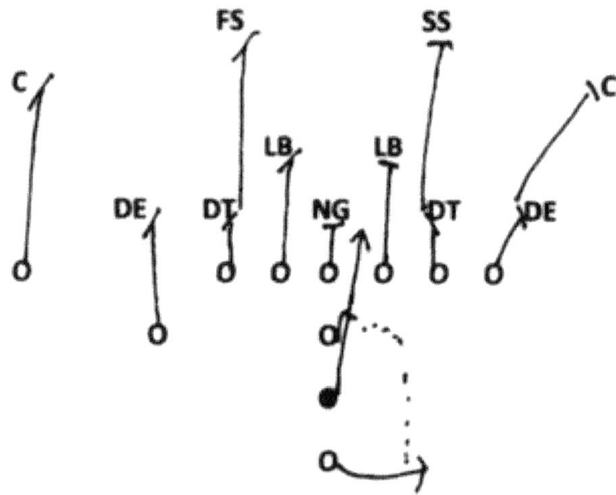

I left 31 dive

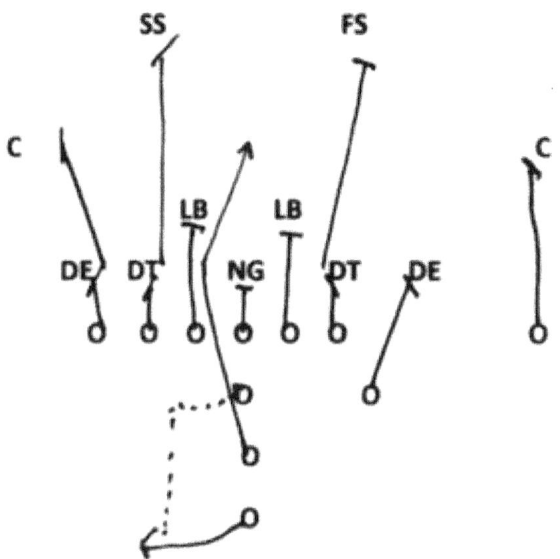

The 23 and 24 Blast

The blast is one of my favorite plays. I've used it over and over to wear down linebackers and pick up first downs. The philosophy on the 23 and 24 blast is to outnumber the other team's blockers in one area. We do this by having our strongside guard and center block down on the nose guard, blowing him out of the hole and walling off his pursuit. The tight end keeps the defensive end from sliding down inside and then goes after the cornerback. Our strongside tackle will seal off the defensive tackle and go get a strong safety. The weakside guard will block the other team's backside linebacker. Our weakside's offensive tackle slows up the backside's defensive tackle and then goes after the free safety. In the backfield the fullback heads for the four hole and blast the play-side linebacker, driving him out of the running lane. The tailback takes a 45-degree open step with his right foot and follows the fullback then receives the handoff from the quarterback. Once the tailback clears the 4 hole at the line of scrimmage, he makes a cut off the fullbacks' block to the outside and down the sideline.

Responsibilities on the 24 and 23 Blast

Tight End

The tight end lines up one yard off the strong tackle's heel. His responsibility on the 23 and 24 blast is to seal off the defensive end's pursuit to the ballcarrier. Most defensive ends will try to come down the line of scrimmage toward the ballcarrier to make a tackle. The tight ends job is to keep this from happening by seal blocking him to the outside. He stays with his block seven counts or until the whistle has blown. If there is no threat to the ballcarrier, he continues and blocks the cornerback. He swings his camera (butt) to the ballcarrier as the play develops.

Strongside Tackle

The strongside tackle seal blocks his man to the outside, turning his camera (butt) to the ballcarrier as the play develops. He lines up one foot off the heel of the strong guard. He uses his basic blocking rule if needed (inside, on, over, and outside) to determine who he will block. The strongside tackle blocks seven counts or until the whistle is blown.

Strongside Guard

The strongside guard lines up one foot off the center's heel. He double-team blocks on the defensive nose guard with the center then releases and walls off the backside linebacker. He blocks seven counts or until the whistle is blown. He keeps his camera (butt) to the ballcarrier sealing off the defensive nose guard.

Center

The center double-team blocks the nose guard with the strong guard. The center and the strong guard turn their cameras (butts) to the hole as the play develops. The strongside guard will slide off to the backside linebacker. They block seven counts or until the whistle is blown.

Weakside Guard

The weakside guard lines up one foot off the heel of the center. His job is to cut off the backside linebacker from the ballcarrier, blocking seven counts or until the whistle blows. He turns his camera (butt) to the ballcarrier as the play develops. If the backside linebacker is not a threat he continues and blocks the strong safety.

Weakside Tackle

The weakside tackle lines up one foot off the heels of the weakside guard. His job is to slow the backside defensive tackle, making him pursue to the outside, then continues and block the free safety. He blocks seven counts or until the whistle is blown, making sure his camera (butt) is turned to the ballcarrier as the play develops.

Slotback

The slotback lines up one yard off the weakside tackle's heel and one yard back. His job is to seal off the backside defensive end or outside linebacker. He blocks seven counts or until the whistle is blown. His camera (butt) is to the ballcarrier has the play develops.

Split End

The split end lines up fifteen yards outside the slotback. The split end job is to stalk block the cornerback and seal him from the ballcarrier. He blocks seven counts or until the whistle is blown. He turns his camera (butt) to the hole as the play develops.

Fullback

The fullback lead blocks through the 4 hole drive blocking the playside linebacker. He lines up three yards behind the quarterback. His block is seven counts or until the whistle is blown. If possible, he would like to block the linebacker to the inside turning his camera (butt) to the hole. The fullback's block is very important for the success of this running play.

Quarterback

The quarterback's number one job is to make a perfect handoff to the tailback. He opens up to his right and hands the ball off to the tailback and fakes a sprint-out action to the play side. Quarterbacks should never look back at the play and give the ballcarrier away.

Tailback

The tailback lines up five yards behind the quarterback. He steps at a forty-five-degree angle toward the four hole and takes the handoff from the quarterback. The tailback follows the fullback through the four hole, making a cut off the fullback's block. We would like to see the tailback cut to the outside and up the sideline.

If you're having trouble with the play-side linebacker, line the slotback in a power I formation and have both the slotback and the fullback double team the play-side linebacker. (The slotback lines up three feet behind the strongside guard)

Example: Play call—(I right, power right, 24 blast)

Points to Remember:

1. *Maintain contact when blocking seven counts.*
2. *The fullback's block is the key to this play's success.*
3. *If you're having trouble blocking the linebacker, shift into power I with the slotback.*
4. *Always turn your camera (butt) to the ballcarrier.*
5. *QB never looks back at the ballcarrier after handoff.*

I left 23 blast

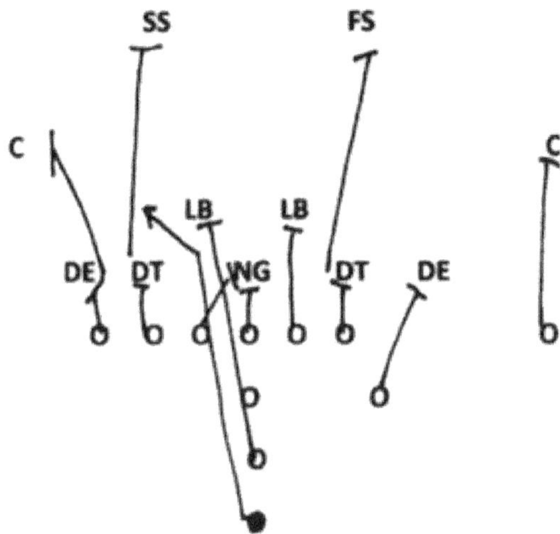

I Right 24 blast

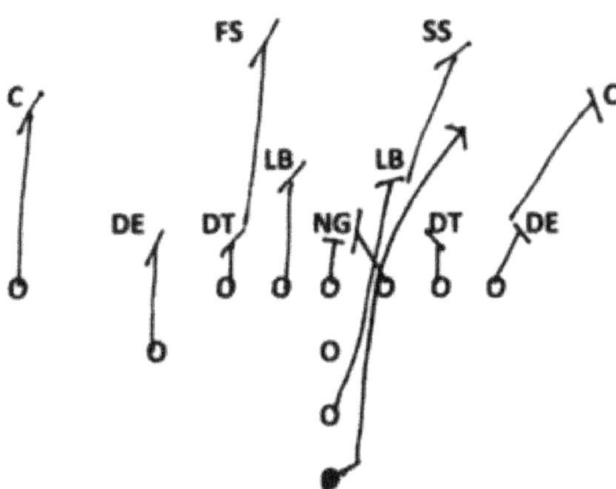

The 25 and 26 Power

The 25 and 26 power running plays have been used in my offense hundreds of times over the years. With the 25 and 26 power, I'm trying to attack the defensive end and overpower the 5 and 6 hole by blocking down on the defensive tackle with my tight end. I then block the defensive end with the fullback going for his inside shoulder and then turning him outside, trying to put the fullback's camera (butt) between him and the ballcarrier. To set up the 25 and 26 power, I always look for the defensive end to line up to far outside the tight end. When this happens, he doesn't close down fast enough to stop the inside running play. This happens because he has trouble stopping the sweep, so he slides out to have a better outside-pursuit angle. That's when we come back inside with the 25 and 26 power. If we find that we're having trouble blocking the defensive end with just the fullback, I will send the slot in motion and hike the ball when the slotback and fullback can double team the defensive end. I can also call, "I right-wing right 26 power." This puts the slotback in a wingback position to help block the defensive end and slid off when the fullback arrives and continues to the cornerback.

Responsibilities for (I Right 26 Power)

Tight End

The tight end will line up one yard outside the offensive tackle. His job is to block down on the defensive tackle and slide off and block the first dangerous man that shows. He will have his camera (butt) to the ballcarrier and will block seven counts or until the whistle is blown.

Strong Tackle

The strong tackle lines up two feet outside the heel of the guard and will double-team block with the tight end on the defensive tackle. He continues to block seven counts and turns his camera (butt) to the ballcarrier as the play develops.

Strong Guard

The strong guard lines up two feet outside the heels of the center and uses his basic blocking rule (inside, on, over, and outside). His block is a seal or cut-off block (probably play-side linebacker). He turns his camera (butt) to the ballcarrier as the play develops. His block is seven counts or until the whistle is blown.

Center

The center refers to his basic blocking rule (inside, on, over, and outside). He uses a seal or cut-off block according to the defensive alignment (probably will block the nose guard) and turns his camera (butt) to the ballcarrier as the play develops. His block is seven counts or until the whistle is blown.

Weak Guard

The weakside guard lines up two feet outside the heel of the center and refers to his basic blocking rule (inside, on, over, and outside). He uses a seal or cut-off block, probably backside linebacker. During the play, he turns his camera (butt) to the ballcarrier as the play develops, seven-count block or until the whistle is blown.

Weakside Tackle

The weakside tackle lines up two feet outside the weakside guard's heels. He refers to his basic blocking rule (inside, on, over, and outside). He uses a cut-off block then scraps off to block the free safety. He always turns his camera (butt) to the ballcarrier as the play develops and continues to block seven counts or until he hears the whistle blown.

Slotback

The slotback sets up one yard outside the weak tackle's heels and one yard deep. His job is to block the backside defensive end or first dangerous man. His block is seven counts or until the whistle is blown. If asked to go in motion he helps double team the play-side defensive end and slides off to cornerback.

Split End

The split end lines up fifteen yards outside the heels of the weakside tackle. He gets downfield and stalk blocks backside cornerback seven counts or until the whistle is blown.

Quarterback

He open steps to his right at a forty-five-degree angle then steps with his left foot then right foot toward the tailback and hands the ball off and carries out the sprint-out fake.

Fullback

The fullback lines up three yards deep behind the QB and open steps and heads toward the defensive end, blocking him inside out. He goes for his inside shoulder and turns him outside away from the ballcarrier, getting his camera (butt) to the ballcarrier as the play develops in a seven-count block or until the whistle is blown.

Tailback (Ballcarrier)

Tailback open steps to his right toward the 6 hole following and reading his fullback's block. He reads his fullback's block by watching the fullback's shoulders to see which shoulder disappears. The tailback cuts to the disappearing shoulder. Once through the hole, he cuts to the outside if he can and heads down the sideline.

Points to Remember:

1. *Run the power when the defensive end is playing too far outside your tight end.*
2. *Run the 25 and 26 power with great blocking and speed, slow-running plays go nowhere.*
3. *Good double-team block by the strong tackle and tight end.*
4. *Tight end, scrap off your double-team block and seal off the strong safety or first threat.*
5. *QB carries out a good sprint-out fake.*
6. *Tailback once through the hole breaks to the outside.*

7. *Remember, Coach, you can call, "I right double tight motion right 26 power." This play call means you will have two tight ends and you're sending your slotback in motion to the right to help the fullback block the defensive end.*

I Right 26 Power

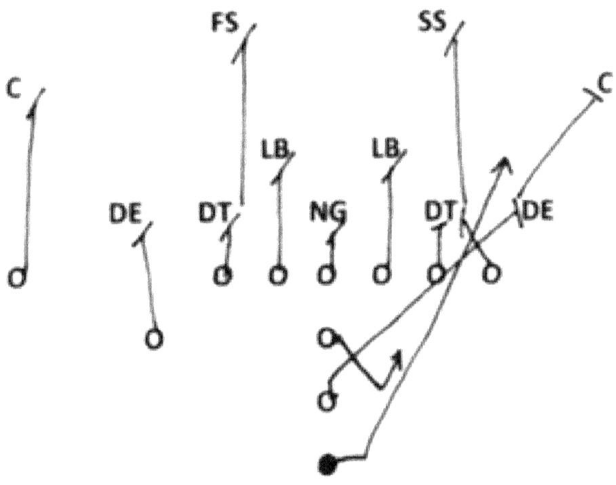

I left 25 power

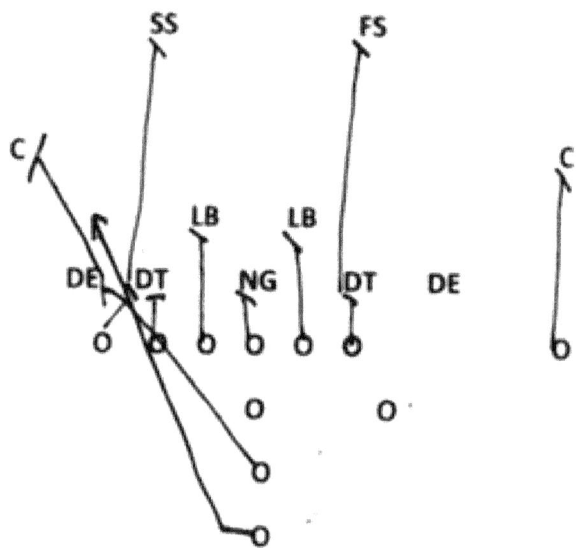

27 and 28 Sweep

When running the sweep, I always look at the defense. I'm looking for certain defensive players to line up in positions that our offensive lineman can take advantage of. I normally set the sweep up by running the football inside with the dive or blast running at the linebackers. I will keep running the football inside until the linebackers step up to stop the inside run, or the defensive end lines up in front or inside the tight end to help his linebackers. Once this happens, I run the ball outside with the 27 or 28 sweep. I'm thinking the defensive linebackers can't get to the outside fast enough to get to the ballcarrier. The strong tackle and tight end help the sweep by clogging up the linebacker's pursuit with their blocks.

Responsibilities

Tight End

The tight end's blocking assignment is to hook the defensive end so he can't pursue to the outside to stop the sweep. If he can't hook him, he goes on to block the corner and the fullback will pick up the defensive. We can also block down with our strongside tackle and defensive end and pull the strongside guard if we need more blocking on the corner.

Offensive Strong Tackle

If our strong tackle is handling the defensive tackle to the sweep side and our tight end can hook the defensive end, then the strongside tackle will call normal. If the tight end can't hook him, then he will call help, and we will block the defensive end with the fullback and pulling guard. The tight end blocks down on the defensive tackle and our offensive tackle would block the play-side linebacker while the strongside guard pulls to help double team the defensive end with the fullback.

Center

Our center will block the nose guard with a seal block turning him away from the ballcarrier and get his camera (butt) to the football. His block is seven counts or until the whistle is blown.

Offensive Guards

Our offensive guards on all offensive plays will always have a two-foot split, but when running the 27 and 28 sweep, we ask all our lineman to cheat in six inches to make the 27 and 28 corner closer and quicker for our tailback to get to. When not pulling on the sweep, most of the time we want our guards to be blocking the play-side linebacker. The golden rule is a seven-count block or until the whistle is blown and his camera (butt) is always to the ballcarrier. If our strongside guard is uncovered, we have the option of pulling him. When we do this, our strongside tackle and tight end will block down.

Weakside Tackle

The weakside offensive tackle lines up two feet off the weakside guard's outside heel. He seal blocks the defensive tackle to his outside and gets upfield to block the free safety.

Split End

Our split end lines up fifteen yards outside the slotback. He seals off the cornerback from the ballcarrier.

QB, Tailback, and Fullback

The quarterback reverse pivots and pitches the ball to the tailback. They both head for the corner, reading the fullback's block. If the fullback blocks the defensive end to the inside, the tailback runs outside. If he blocks the defensive end outside, then the tailback cuts to the inside. We teach our offensive backs when running the football to read the blocker's shoulder that disappears. We know that whatever shoulder disappears gives you the direction to make your cut. The quarterback helps with blocking on the corner.

Slotback

I also can move the slot over to the tight-end side as a wingback or send him in motion toward the tight to block the cornerback. Here's a play call example number 1—I right motion 28 sweep. We would have motioned and hiked the ball on the QB's command when the slotback gets in position. Here's example number 2—I right wing 28 sweep. There would be no motion; the slotback would simply line up to the tight-end side as a wingback.

Points to Remember:

1. *I've watched a lot of teams run the sweep, and they run it to slow.*
2. *To make a quicker and better pitch, QB should turn around or open up far enough to lead the tailback with his pitch.*
3. *I teach a firm pitch not too hard and not too soft. Don't start the pitch too low; it will come up to high.*

4. *The tailback should be four yards deep and four yards in front of the QB when he receives the pitch.*

5. *Great pitches help to generate great sweeps and don't slow up the ballcarrier.*

6. *Tailbacks need to get to the corner with speed and turn up the field.*

7. *We also need a great block by our tight end or fullback on the defensive end.*

REMEMBER SLOW SWEEPS GO NOWHERE! *I push the players to run our sweeps with lightning speed and determined seven-count blocks.*

I Right 28 sweep

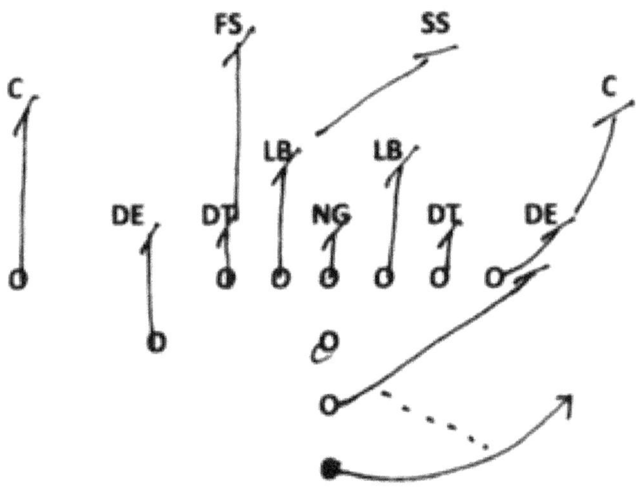

I left sweep Left

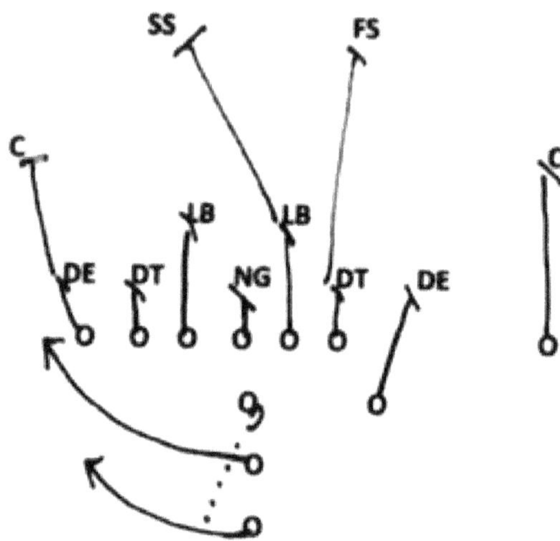

I right 28 sweep help call

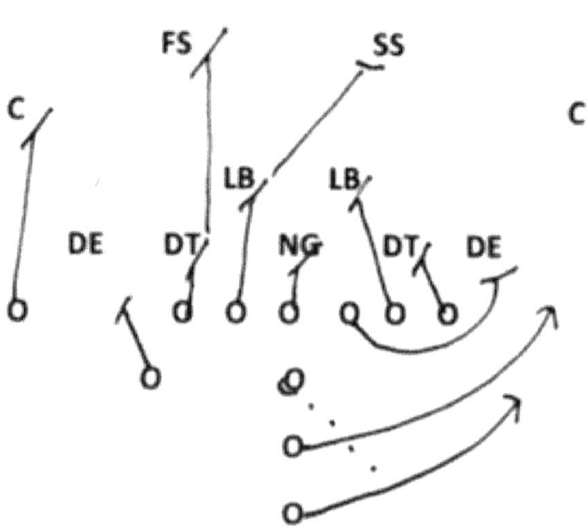

I left 27 sweep help call

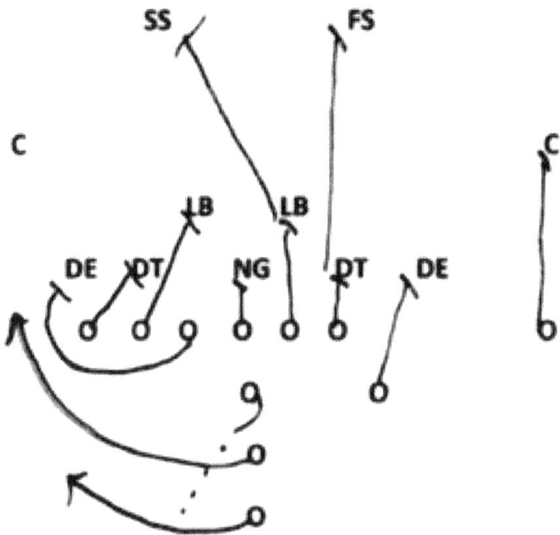

The 23 and 24 Counter

The 23 and 24 counter is a very effective play when called at the right time. The counter is set up by running the football in one direction over and over, getting the defense to over-pursue. I watch during a game and decide how they're pursuing the first half. If they have started to over-pursue, I will wait for the start of the second half and run the 23 and 24 blast a few more times then come back with the 23 and 24 counter. This catches the defense out of position, and to their surprise, our tailback starts one direction and cuts back the other. It completely catches the defense by surprise and many times can lead to big yardage and once in a while a touchdown. The counter must be set up and used at the right moment. If your inside running plays like the 23 and 24 blast are making yardage and the backside linebacker tries to help the play-side linebacker by leaving his responsibility early, then the counter should work. Once in a while, I will run the counter to keep the defensive linebackers at home longer and to slow down their pursuit; this can help the 23 and 24 blast work better. The important piece for running the counter is the fullback filling quickly for the pulling guard and then the tailback selling his first step and cutting to the opposite direction. For the counter to be effective, our lineman must pull quickly and be good trap blockers. They must stay with their block until the whistle is blown and not give away which defensive player they're going to block. One more thing, make sure your linemen have their cameras (butts) to the ballcarrier as the play develops.

Responsibilities on the 23 Counter (for Example of Play Call—I Right 23 Counter)

Tight End

The tight end will line up one yard outside the strong tackle. His job is to seal block the defensive end's pursuit to the ballcarrier. He should be turning his camera (butt) to the ballcarrier as the play develops and block his man seven counts or until the whistle is blown.

Strongside Tackle

The strongside tackle will line up two feet off the strongside guard's heel. He uses his basic blocking rule inside, on, over, and outside. His job is to seal block his defensive man's (defensive tackle) pursuit to the football. When blocking, he should turn his camera (butt) to the ballcarrier as the play develops and block his man seven counts or until the whistle is blown.

Strongside Guard

The strongside guard will pull to his left then turn up in the 3 hole and block the play-side linebacker. He lines up two feet off the heel of the center. He needs to block his man out of the 3 hole for seven counts or until the whistle is blown. The tailback makes his cut depending on which direction the strong guard blocks his man.

Center

The center's number one job is to get the ball to the quarterback.

He then seal blocks the backside linebacker seven counts or until the whistle is blown. His camera (butt) should be turned toward the ballcarrier as the play develops.

Weakside Guard

The weakside guard lines up two feet off the heel of the center. His job is to block down on the nose guard and seal off his pursuit to the ballcarrier. His block is seven counts or until the whistle is blown. His camera (butt) should turn toward the ballcarrier as the play develops.

Weakside Tackle

The weakside tackle lines up two feet off the heel of the weakside guard. His job is to use his basic blocking rule (inside, on, over, and outside) and seal blocks his man's (defensive tackle) pursuit to the football. His block is seven counts or until the whistle is blown. He turns his camera (butt) to the ballcarrier as the play develops.

Slotback

The slot lines up one yard outside the weak tackle and one yard deep. His job is to seal block the defensive end or outside linebacker's pursuit to the ballcarrier. His block is seven counts or until the whistle is blown. He turns his camera (butt) to the ballcarrier as he blocks and drives his man away from the hole.

Split End

The split end lines up fifteen yards outside the slotback. His job is to stalk block the cornerback's pursuit to the football. He blocks for seven counts or until the whistle is blown. When blocking his camera (butt), he turns toward the ballcarrier.

Fullback

Fullbacks need to make a good ball fake with the quarterback and quickly fill for the pulling guard. He helps with the center to cut off the backside linebacker's pursuit to the football. His block is seven counts or until the whistle is blown. He needs to turn his camera (butt) to the ballcarrier as the play develops.

Quarterback

The quarterback's number one job is to make a quick fake to the fullback's pivot and hands off the football to the tailback clean. The quarterback should always fake a sprint-out action in case we call a play-action pass or quarterback keep. The quarterback should never look back at the running back and give the ballcarrier away.

Tailback

The tailback's number one job is to hit the hole. His job is to open step to his right and fake the 4 hole then cut back to the 3 hole. Once through the line of scrimmage, he cuts to the outside or inside according to his strongside guard's block. His job is to hold on to the ball until the whistle is blown.

Points to Remember:

1. *Set up the counter by running the blast or sweep then coming back later with the 24 and 23 counter.*
2. *Trap blocking must be practiced to become effective; deception is everything.*
3. *The lineman stays with your block seven counts and turn your camera (butt) to the ballcarrier.*
4. *The fullback fills for the pulling guard quickly.*
5. *The quarterback's number one job is a good hand fake to the fullback and then a good handoff to the tailback.*
6. *The quarterback on the 23 counter opens to the fullback on the right faking a handoff using his left hand and then gives the football to the tailback on the cut back with his right hand.*
7. *The tailback sells your first two steps. Open step right with a good head fake then cut back left following the strongside guard on the counter.*

I right 23 counter

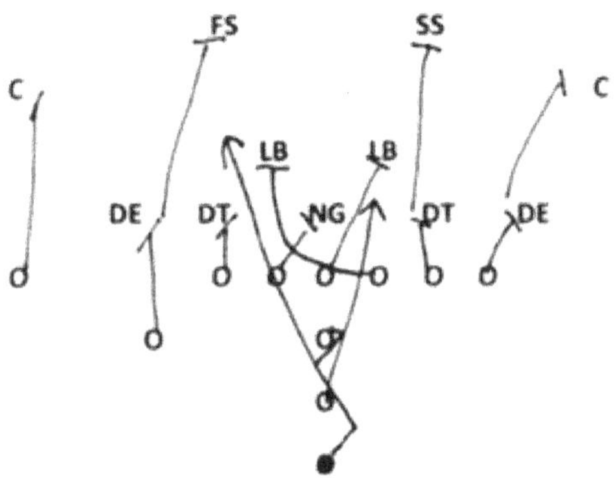

I left 24 counter

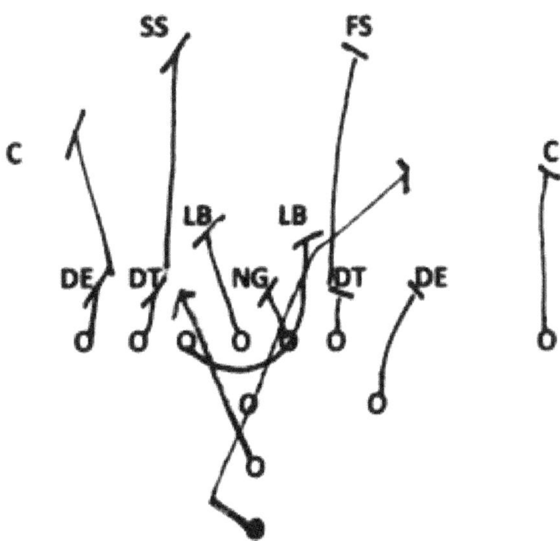

CHAPTER 6
Pass Offense

Passing the Football

Passing the football over the years, I've found that throwing to one receiver has been successful. By throwing to the main target, we know where the football is going. To help our primary receiver, we run clearing patterns to clear the target area of defenders. If our main receiver is covered, we will look for other receivers to be open or simply keep it and run. My feeling is that passing the football plays a major role in winning football games. It keeps the defense honest and gives us the opportunity to gain good yardage and spreads out the defense.

I have used three types of passes during the years depending on the age group I'm coaching. My first passing package would be play-action off our running plays. The younger your players, the more effective the play-action pass will be. I found younger defensive players fly to the ballcarrier wanting to make the big play and leave their pass responsibilities to early, knowing these coaches will take advantage of their play-action passes by faking a run and throwing the pass. My second package is the roll-out pass. We throw the ball on the run rolling out looking for a receiver or attacking the line of scrimmage, reading the pass defense, and running if they stay with the receiver. The quarterback always has the option to run the football. Then my last package would be the straight drop-back pass. These passing packages are used depending on the strengths of our quarterback. I try to keep the passing as simple as possible and not throw interceptions. When using the play-action pass, the ability to fool the other team by the quarterback faking a handoff is essential to the success of your pass plays. When rolling out, the quarterback's ability to attack the line of scrimmage by running with the ball making the defensive backs come up to stop him is crucial. Last if you have a tall quarterback who is able to see over the line of scrimmage and can find his receivers, then the drop-back pass becomes very effective. Whichever one you use, keep it simple to help keep from throwing interceptions.

Scramble Right and Left

The scramble right and left pass are pass plays my high school coach ran back in sixties at Sunset High School in Beaverton, Oregon. At that time, I played fullback and nose guard for the Apollos, and we had just acquired a new football coach who loved the run-and-shoot offense. The scramble right and left pass gave our passing attack the ability to flood an area of the field, making it hard for the defense to defend our receivers. We would split our ends out fifteen yards. Our slotbacks would line up outside the tackle and one yard off the line of scrimmage. The linemen increase their splits to two feet, and when the football was hiked, they would take one fire step forward and pass block. If we were running a scramble-right pass, our left slot went in motion when the quarterback raised his heel. When the motion back reached the desired location, the quarterback would ask for the football and roll out to his right, passing on the run while squaring his shoulders to line of scrimmage and throwing off his outside foot. Our fullback would run toward the defensive end and seal block him from the quarterback. The motion back would run upfield toward the strong safety on a go pattern. Our play-side slot would do an out pattern at ten yards toward the sideline. The play-side split end ran a go pattern down the sideline to take the cornerback with him. There wouldn't be anybody that could cover the play-side slot on the down out pattern. If the corner came up to cover him, our quarterback would throw down the sideline to the split end. It's a simple read by the quarterback but needs to be practice.

Responsibilities

Play-Side Split End
The play-side split end lines up fifteen yards outside the tackle. His job is to run a go pattern up the sideline, taking the cornerback with him. If the cornerback doesn't go with him, he continues his pattern and looks for the football ball to be thrown to him.

Strongside Tackle
The strongside tackle takes one fire step forward and pass blocks. He turns his camera (butt) to the football as the play develops. He blocks seven counts or until the whistle is blown.

Strongside Guard
The strongside guard takes on fire step forward and pass blocks. He

turns his camera (butt) to the football as the play develops. He blocks seven counts or until the whistle blows.

Center

The center's number one job is to have a perfect exchange when hiking the football. He then sets up and pass blocks, turning his camera (butt) to the football as the play develops. He blocks seven counts or until the whistle is blown.

Weakside Guard

The weakside guard takes one fire step forward and pass blocks, turning his camera (butt) to the football has the play develops. He blocks seven counts or until the whistle is blown.

Weakside Tackle

The weakside tackle takes one fire step forward and pass blocks, turning his camera (butt) to the football as the play develops. He blocks seven counts or until the whistle is blown.

Slotback

The slotback goes in motion, on the centers snap turns up field on a go pattern.

Backside Split End

The backside split end sets up fifteen yards outside the weak tackle. He runs a go pattern, taking the cornerback with him.

Fullback

The fullback open steps toward the defensive end and blocks him outside in and seals him off from the quarterback. He turns his camera to the football as the play develops. He blocks seven counts or until the whistle blows.

Quarterback

The quarterback sends the left slot in motion by raising his left heel and asks for the football when the left slotback is off the hip of the right slotback. He rolls out to the right, squaring his shoulders up to the line of scrimmage and passing the football off his outside foot to the slotback on an out pattern. If he is covered, the quarterback looks downfield at the play-side split end or tucks the ball and runs.

Points to Remember:

1. *Run the motion quickly so the defense has trouble adjusting.*
2. *The fullback needs to be a good blocker on the defensive end.*
3. *The quarterback throws off the outside foot and squares his shoulders to the line of scrimmage.*
4. *Receivers run good sharp routes.*
5. *The quarterback knows your reads.*

Scramble right pass

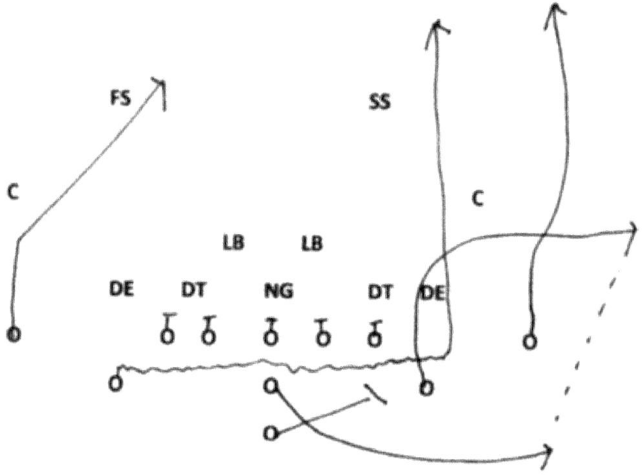

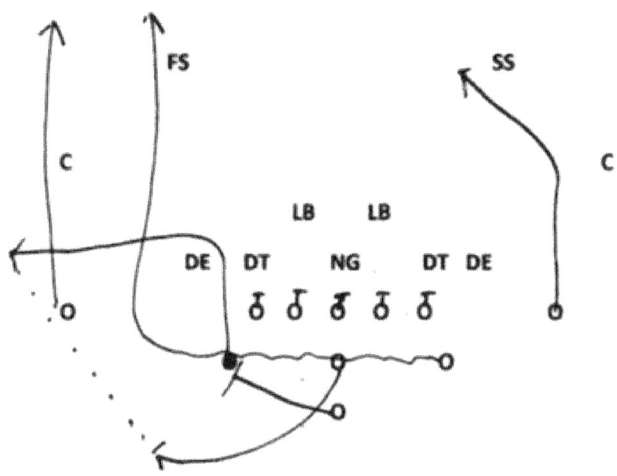

The Tight-End Dump

The tight-end dump pass is used when the linebackers are way up in the box trying to stop the fullback dive or the blast. The idea is for the quarterback to simply dump a quick pass over the lineman and heads to the tight end for ten yards. Sometimes to the surprise of everyone, the tight end breaks loose and goes for six points. It's a very quick pass after the ball is snapped. All the other players fire out one step and pass block. There's really not much time for anything else. The real key to this pass play is the position of the linebackers and if there is a real lane or opening for the tight end to catch the ball. Also the quarterback must be careful how the ball is thrown. I've always loved the tight-end dump; sometimes it's been a great play to back off the linebackers. If I'm going to use the dump, it must be practiced for perfection or it can be bad news.

Responsibilities

Tight End

The tight end will widen out his stance a good six inches when he lines up to help push the defensive end out, giving himself a bigger lane to catch the ball. His job is to slant behind the linebackers and in front of the strong safety to catch the dump pass. His stance is balanced so he won't give away where he is going. He looks straight ahead never looking at the slant pattern until the ball is snapped.

Strong Tackle

The strong tackle takes a fire step and sets up to pass block.

Strong Guard

The strong guard takes a fire step and sets up to pass block.

Center

The center snaps the ball perfectly and sets up to pass block.

Weak Guard

The weak guard takes a fire step, sets up to pass block.

Weak Tackle

The weak tackle takes a fire step and sets up to pass block.

Slotback

The slotback takes an open step toward the outside to distract strong safety.

Split End

The split end takes a step to his outside to get the cornerback's attention.

Fullback

The fullback open steps right if it's a slant right and fakes a dive.

Tailback

The tailback open steps left if it's a slant right and blocks left.

Quarterback

The quarterback receives the football from the center, quickly fakes a quick handoff to the right stand's tall, and dumps the football to the tight end.

Points to Remember:

1. *The tight end widens out your stance.*
2. *Don't look at your pass route and give it away.*
3. *Run a 45-degree slant.*
4. *The quarterback fakes a quick handoff, stands up, and passes the football firmly, not hard, not soft but firm.*
5. *Don't throw a dump pass unless linebackers are up.*

I right tight end dump

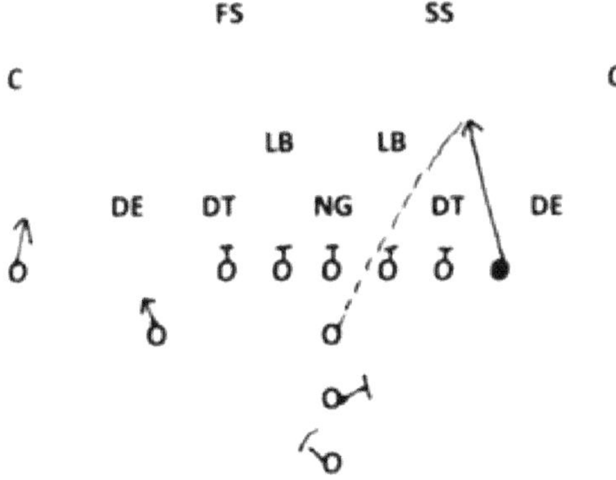

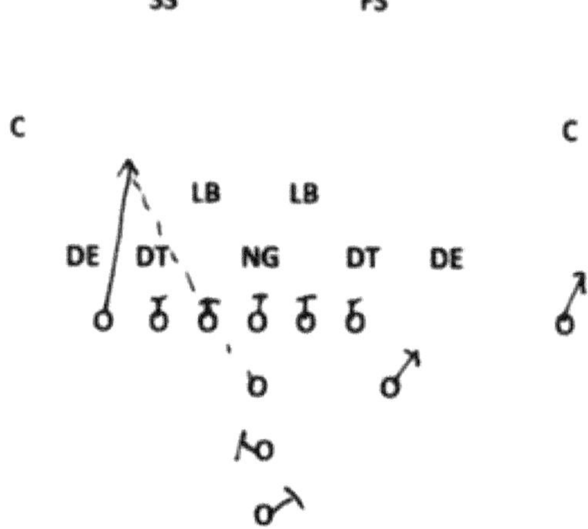

36 and 35 Power Pass

The power pass is a play-action pass that has been effective over the years. It earns its value from gaining yards on the ground by running the 36 and 35 power and making the defense work hard to stop it. Once again the defenders will start leaving their pass responsibilities to pursue the ballcarrier.

Using the same look like the run, the fullback will head toward the defensive end to block; this time he continues and runs by on a pass pattern toward the sideline. The tailback is taking a fake handoff from the quarterback and then blocks the defensive end. After faking the handoff, the quarterback continues to roll out to the play side, hiding the football on his hip. The line pass blocks while the other receivers are running pass patterns to help clear out the defensive backs. The quarterback passes the football to the fullback if he's open; if not, he tucks the ball and runs upfield. During the play, the defensive corner will have come up to help stop the run. If he does, the fullback should be wide open.

Responsibilities

Tight End
The tight end's responsibility is to seal down toward the defensive tackle then release on a flag pattern toward the strong safety to take him out of the fullback's pattern.

Strongside Tackle
The strongside tackle pass blocks seven counts, turning his camera (butt) to the football as the play develops. He blocks seven counts or until the whistle is blown.

Strongside Guard
The strongside guard pass blocks and turns his camera (butt) to the ball as the play develops. He blocks seven counts or until the whistle is blown.

Center
The center snaps the football to the quarterback then pass blocks and turns his camera (butt) to the ball as the play develops. He blocks seven counts or until the whistle is blown.

Weakside Guard
The weakside guard pass blocks and turns his camera (butt) to the play as the play develops. He blocks seven counts or until the whistle is blown.

Weakside Tackle
The weakside tackle pass blocks and turns his camera (butt) to the play as the play develops. He blocks seven counts or until the whistle is blown.

Split End

The split end runs a post pattern until the whistle is blown.

Slotback

The slotback runs a post pattern taking the free safety out of the play until the whistle is blown.

Fullback

The fullback open steps toward the defensive end like he is blocking then continues on a pass pattern ten yards out and toward the sideline. He is the number one receiver to catch the football.

Tailback

The tailback open steps to the hole, takes a fake handoff from the quarterback, and then blocks the defensive end to his inside. He pass blocks and turns his camera (butt) to the quarterback as the play develops. He blocks seven counts or until the whistle is blown.

Quarterback

The quarterback receives the ball from the center, opens at a forty-five-degree angle, faking a handoff to his tailback. He then hides the football on his hip and rolls out to the play side, looking to pass the ball to the fullback on a ten-yard down-and-out pattern. If the fullback is covered, he tucks the ball and runs.

Points to Remember:

1. *Make sure the defense is coming up to stop the run.*
2. *Good fake handoff.*
3. *Good block by the tailback.*
4. *Fullback catches the ball then runs first.*
5. *Slow plays go nowhere.*

I left 35 power pass

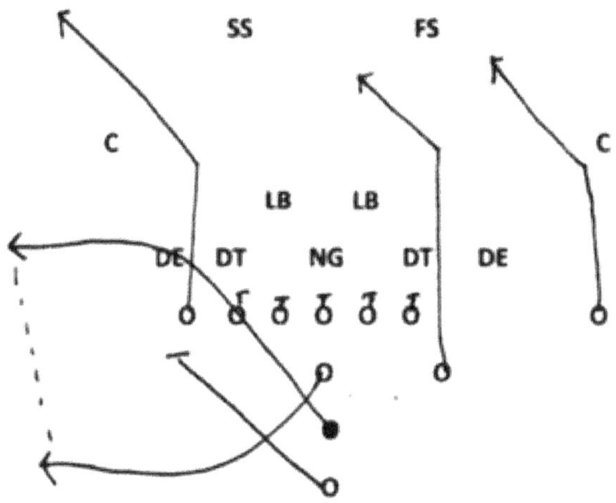

I right 36 power pass

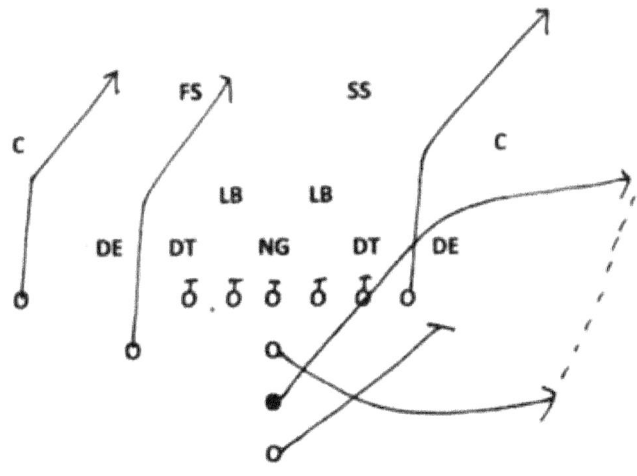

Play Action 27 and 28 Sweep Pass

Looking back over the years coaching the sweep pass has brought many exciting moments because of its deception. The success of the sweep pass comes from running the sweep successfully and then to everyone's surprise, your tailback stops, sets up, and passes the ball to your tight-end downfield. Some might ask the question, why would you want to throw a pass to your tight end and not a wide receiver? Here's my answer. For this play to be successful, you must first sell the sweep pass by running the sweep. When the defensive players truly believe your sweep is effective they will leave their responsibilities early and pursue the ballcarrier. When you see they have committed to stopping the sweep, that's when it's time for the sweep pass to the tight end. The tight end will do a great job influence blocking down on the defensive tackle for three counts then releasing on his pass pattern. The defensive corner by that time will have read sweep and come up to help contain the corner. Our tight end will have slipped out behind him. As this is happening, the slotback will run a pass pattern at the strong safety, leading him away from the tight end's pass route. The tight end's pattern should be wide open. Some teams make the mistake of not selling the influence block by the tight end; they release a receiver downfield too early without really selling the sweep. If you're going to use the sweep pass, then moving the football using the 27 and 28 sweep is a must. If your sweep isn't effective, then the defense won't over-pursue correctly.

Responsibilities (27 and 28 Sweep Pass)

Tight End

The tight end will influence block down on the defensive tackle in three counts then release at a forty-five-degree angle toward the sideline. His release should take him behind the defensive corner's pursuit of the ballcarrier. He is the number one target on the sweep pass.

Strongside Tackle

The strongside tackle pass blocks to the sweep side, turning his camera (butt) to the passer as the play develops. He blocks seven counts or until the whistle is blown.

Strongside Guard

The strongside guard pass blocks to the sweep side, turning his camera (butt) to the passer as the play develops. He blocks seven counts or until the whistle is blown.

Center

The center pass blocks to the sweep side, turning his camera (butt) to the passer as the play develops. He blocks seven counts or until the whistle is blown.

Weak Guard

The weak guard pass blocks, turning his camera(butt) to the passer as the play develops. He blocks seven counts or until the whistle is blown.

Weak Tackle

The weak tackle pass blocks, turning his camera (butt) to the passer as the play develops. He blocks seven counts or until the whistle is blown.

Slotback

The slotback runs a post pattern toward the strong safety. He tries to get the strong safety to cover him.

Fullback

The fullback open steps toward the defensive end, cutting him off from the tailback and blocking him outside in. He blocks, turning his camera (butt) to the ballcarrier as the play develops. His block is seven counts or until the whistle is blown.

Tailback

Tailback open steps toward the play side and receives the pitch from the quarterback. He heads for the corner, selling the sweep and staying five yards deep. He reads the defensive cornerback and if the cornerback attacks him, he sets up and passes to the tight end. If the cornerback stays back, he tucks the ball and runs the football.

QB

The quarterback reverse pivots and pitches the football to the tailback then blocks for the sweep.

Points to Remember:

1. *To run the sweep pass, your 27 and 28 sweep run must be effective or the defense won't over-pursue the ballcarrier.*
2. *Your tight end must do a great job on acting out his influence block on the defensive tackle or his release won't be clean.*
3. *The fullback must be aggressive, blocking the defensive end and keeping him off the tailback.*
4. *The tailback must have the ability to complete the pass.*
5. *Sell the sweep.*

I Right 28 sweep pass delay

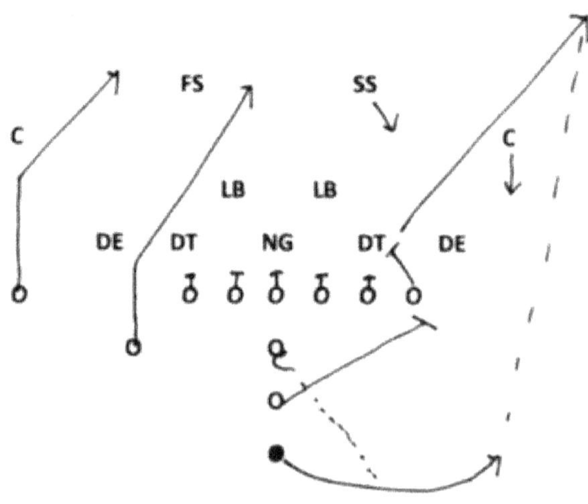

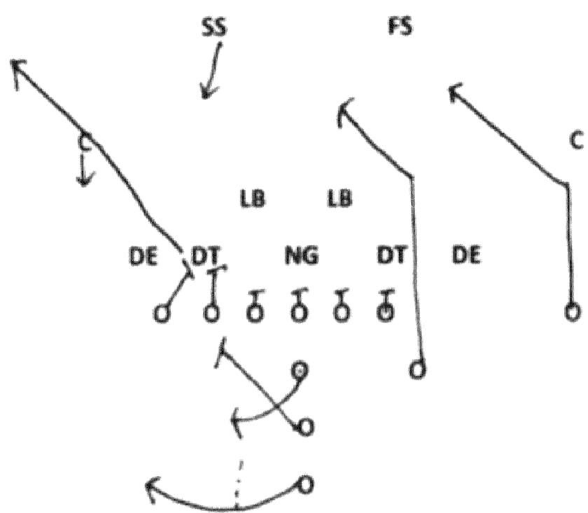

The Slant Pass

The slant pass is very effective when the defensive corners are playing back too far or outside the receiver. This pass play is a quick throw to your split end after he starts with one step straight upfield then planting his outside foot to cut back toward the middle. The quarterback hits him right after the cut, so he doesn't slow him down. The defensive backs don't have enough time to react to stop the pass because it's so quick. This also takes the rest of the defense out of the play. When you use this pass, make sure you don't throw the football too high, and it ends up being intercepted by the cornerback.

Responsibilities

Tight End
The tight end takes one fire step forward and pass blocks. He blocks seven counts or until the whistle is blown while turning his camera (butt) to the football as the play develops.

Strongside Tackle

The strongside tackle takes one fire step forward and pass blocks seven counts or until the whistle is blown. He turns his camera (butt) to the football as the play develops.

Strongside Guard

The strongside guard takes a fire one step forward and pass blocks seven counts or until the whistle is blown. He turns his camera to the football as the play develops.

Center

The center's number one job is to deliver a perfect snap to the quarterback on the correct count. After the snap, he pass blocks seven counts or until the whistle is blown. He keeps his camera (butt) to the football.

Weakside Guard

The weakside takes one fire step forward and pass blocks seven counts or until the whistle is blown. He turns his camera (butt) to the football as the play develops.

Weakside Tackle

The weakside tackle takes one fire step forward and pass blocks seven counts or until the whistle is blown. He turns his camera (butt) to the football as the play develops.

Slotback

Slotback pass blocks the back side rush.

Split End

The split end releases one step forward and drives the cornerback, back then cuts at a forty-five-degree angle toward the middle. He looks for the pass from the quarterback right after his cut and turns upfield.

Fullback

The fullback open steps to his left and pass blocks seven counts or until the whistle is blown. He protects the quarterback from being hit.

Tailback

The tailback takes an open step to his right and pass blocks seven counts or until the whistle is blown. He protects the quarterback from being hit.

Quarterback

The quarterback receives the snap from the center and takes one step back. He squares his shoulders to the split end and passes the ball. His pass is quick and aimed at the waist of his split.

Points to Remember:

1. *You must have a good snap from the center.*
2. *The quarterback must have a quick, accurate release.*
3. *The quarterback must have good lead time when throwing the slot pass.*
4. *The split end when he releases must drive the cornerback with his first step before his cut.*
5. *Catch the football!*

I right slant pass left

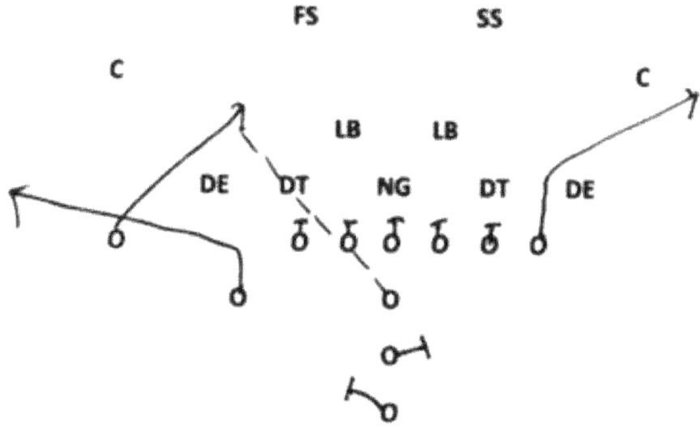

I left slant pass right

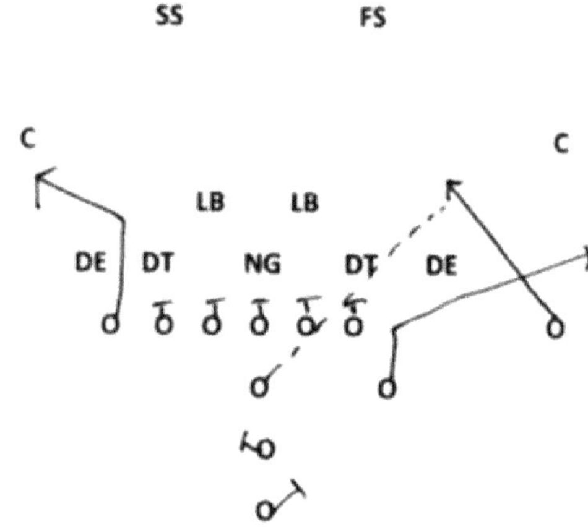

Drop-Back Pass 50 Series

I use the drop-back pass when I have a quarterback that has the arm to throw the long pass and has the ability to deliver it. During my early years of coaching, I had one young quarterback as a freshman that could not only drop back but pass the football fifty yards down the field with pinpoint accuracy. That doesn't happen very often. That same quarterback went on to lead his high school to the 1980 Oregon 5A football state title. The rest of the team was big and talented, and they were a real threat to anyone who played them. My point is this, some teams can throw and some can't. Evaluate what you do best and don't waste a lot of time in practice throwing the ball down the field if you can't.

The 50 series passing plays are designed for a five-step drop-back pass. It's used for players that can pass the football and are accurate. Coaches realize young quarterbacks are still growing and not quite ready for the long fifty-yard bomb, so they throw the short 50s fifty passes like the short ten-yard hook pattern, or they might use the scramble pass plays. Whatever you decide to throw, keep it within your quarterback's abilities. When using long 50s pass plays, your quarterback will drop back five steps, keeping his eyes on the field in front of him. When he finds his receiver, he needs to make a decision whether or not to pass the football. If he doesn't like what he sees, he'll check off to a second receiver or tuck the ball and run. If the quarterback checks off to a second receiver, I would like that second receiver easy to find. Our offensive line in the 50 series simple pass blocks, forming a cup around the quarterback. Our tackles will ride their blocks to the outside so the quarterback can step up in the pocket to pass or run. Our guards would like to hold the inside rush up or ride their blocks to the outside to help break down the containment lanes. We don't want the quarterback to be touched during any passing play.

Quarterbacks need to spend extra hours practicing with the receivers running sharp routes and getting the timing down in order to be successful using the fifty pass plays. Knowing when and where your receivers will be and coaching good pass blocking can be a real advantage in passing the football.

Tight-End 50 Hook

The tight end lines up one yard outside the strong tackle. His job is to run a sharp hook at ten yards. He makes his cut to the inside coming back two steps to the quarterback, making eye contact and ready to catch the football.

Strong Tackle

The strong tackle pass blocks and protects the quarterback from the outside pass rush. He pass blocks seven counts or until the whistle is blown, keeping his camera (butt) to the football as the play develops. He protects the quarterback from being hit or sacked.

The Strongside Guard

The strongside guard pass blocks and protects the quarterback from the inside rush and from being hit or sacked. He blocks seven counts or until the whistle is blown, keeping his camera (butt) to the quarterback as the play develops.

The Center

The center pass blocks and protects the quarterback from the inside pass rush, protecting the quarterback from getting sacked. He blocks seven counts or until the whistle is blown keeping his camera (butt) to the hole as the play develops.

The Weakside Guard

The weakside guard pass blocks and protects the quarterback from the inside rush being sacked. He blocks seven counts or until the whistle is blown, keeping his camera (butt) to the quarterback as the play develops.

The Weakside Tackle

The weakside tackle pass blocks and protects the quarterback from the outside rush and being sacked. He blocks seven counts or until the whistle is blown keeping his camera (butt) to the quarterback as the play develops.

Slotback

The slotback goes in motion and turns upfield when the football is snapped. He drives the cornerback, running a sharp hook pattern to the inside at ten yards and looks back toward the quarterback for eye contact. He is ready to catch the football.

Split End

The split end drives the defensive cornerback, running a sharp hook pattern to the inside at ten yards. He turns back toward the quarterback, making eye contact and looking to catch the football.

Fullback

The fullback open steps toward the defensive end to the play side. He blocks the defensive end seven counts or until the whistle is blown. He turns his camera (butt) to the quarterback as the play develops. He keeps the quarterback from being hit or sacked.

Tailback

The tailback open steps to his left and is ready to block the defensive end to the split end side. If there is no pass rush from the defensive end, he releases on a swing pattern ready to catch the football. If the defensive-end pass rushes, the tailback stays home and blocks him seven counts or until the whistle is blown. He protects the quarterback from being hit or sacked. He turns his camera (butt) to the quarterback as the play develops.

Quarterback

Good five-step drop, set up find your receiver. If he's not open, check off to another receiver or hit the tailback on swing pattern. The last option is to run the football.

Responsibilities for the 51 and 52 Cross

Tight End

The tight end runs a ten-yard flag pattern.

Slotback

The slotback goes into motion. When the football is snapped, he runs a ten-post pattern.

Split End

The split end runs a ten-yard shallow post pattern.

Points to Remember:

1. *Good fake on your pass patterns.*
2. *The quarterback spends extra time working on patterns.*
3. *Line, be determined on pass blocking.*
4. *No holding penalties.*

5.   *The quarterback makes a good five-step drop.*

I left 50 hook pass

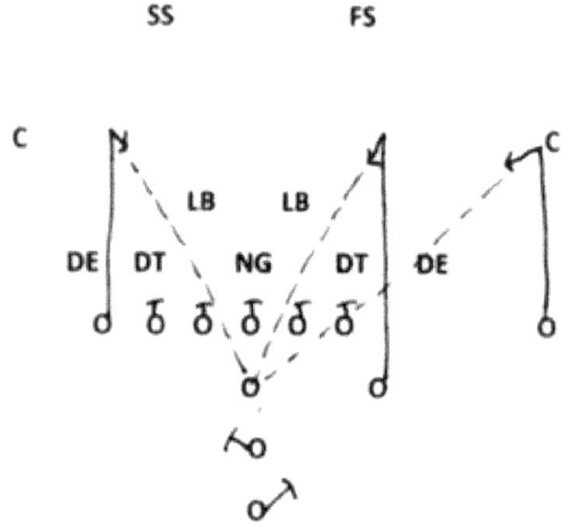

I right 50 hook pass

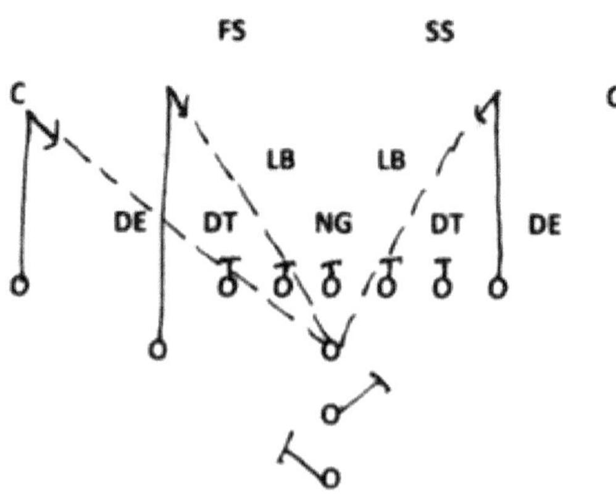

I right 50 motion cross

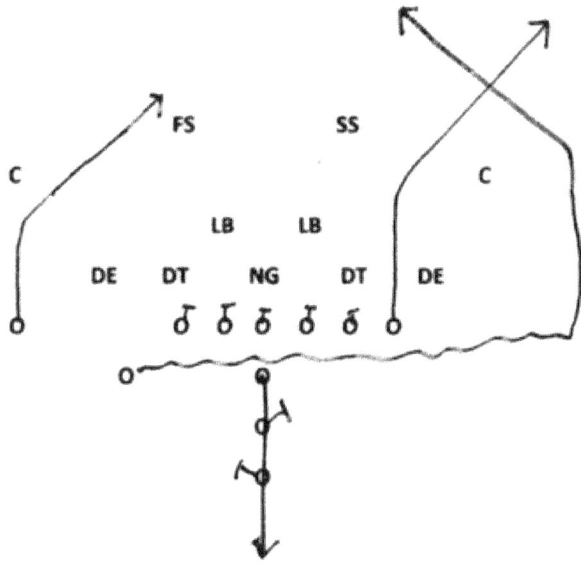

I left 50 motion cross

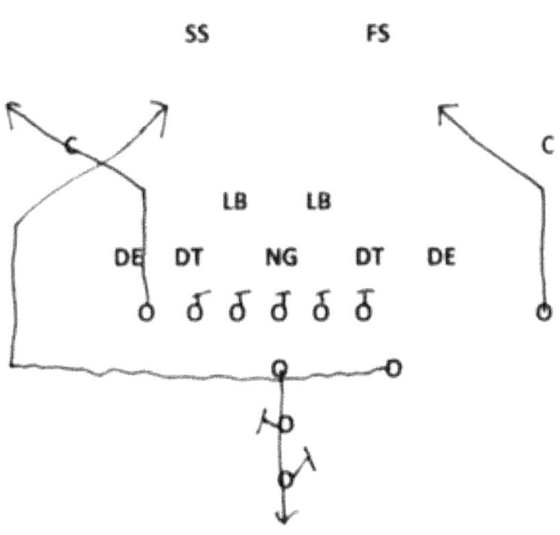

I right 50 go pass

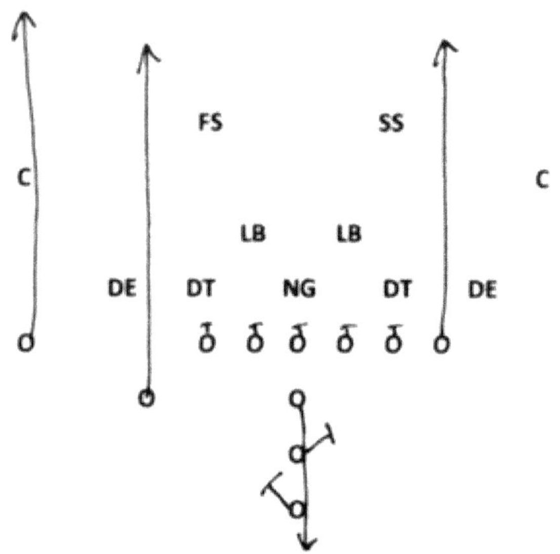

I left 50 go pass

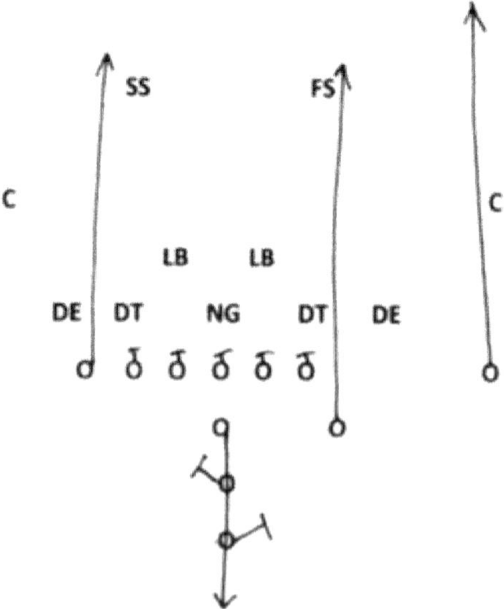

CHAPTER 7
Offensive Drills

Offensive Line Drills

Offensive Line Stance and Starts

This drill is done on the goal line. The players form four lines facing the football field. The first player in each line sets up on the goal line in an offensive stance three yards between the other lineman. The other players wait their turn in line a few yards back. The coach is out front giving the cadence to start the drill. On the coach's count, the first four offensive linemen fire out straight ahead for five yards then circle back and get in line. After all the players have gone through a number of times, the coach will ask for a five-count double-team block. The two players on the right will work together to simulate a double-team block and the two players on the left will do the same. On the coach's command, both double teams fire out for five yards. After all the players have gone through the double-team block a number of times, the coach will ask for a pull block right or left down the line, in which all four players will pull down the line in the same direction at the same time. The coach will end the drill with form-pass blocking. When simulating pass blocking, players will get into a pass-block position from their offensive stance; they will retreat two or three yards to simulate taking on the defensive rush. This drill is a form and position blocking only.

Points to Remember:

1. *Everyone gets off the football at the same time.*
2. *Use good form and get in a good position on blocks.*
3. *This drill can be used with player's step by step for position blocking.*

Pulling Down the Line

This drill is done on the goal line. Form four lines facing the football field. The first player in each line sets up in an offensive stance five yards apart from the other lineman on the goal line. The other players wait their turn in line a few yards back. The coach places a cone five yards to the right of the lineman and another cone ten yards downfield in line with the first cone. The coach stands in front of the drill facing the players. He calls out the cadence, and on his count, all four linemen open step and pull down the line going around the cone, running ten yards downfield and lining up to come back on the second cone. The coach continues until everyone has pulled to the right. Upon coming back the other way, the coach will have the players pull to the left and go around the cone, setting up once again on the goal line.

Points to Remember:

1. *The linemen should open step toward the direction they are pulling.*
2. *Don't lean or point in your stance.*
3. *This drill is run at lightning speed.*
4. *Go through the drill at least three times.*

Pulling Down the Line

Sled Drill

The blocking sled is used to get the offensive line to work as a single unit coming off the line of scrimmage when the ball is snapped. It also builds strength in the legs and back and teaches the players to stay low while blocking. The players will line up on the sled according to the position they play. The coach will give the snap count, and the players will drive the sled seven counts down the field. If they do a good job, the sled will go straight because the players are blocking together. If the sled turns to one side or another, then you know someone started to slow down and hit the sled too late, and the blocking is uneven. If the players don't stay low, the front of the sled will dig into the grass and it's hard to move. If players are working as a team and in the correct blocking position, the sled will slide down the field in a straight line easily as they all work together. The sled is a great drill and I believe it helps players work as a unit.

Points to Remember:

1. *The sled develops, getting off the ball together.*
2. *The sled can build strength in your lineman.*
3. *The sled helps develop a good blocking form.*

Offensive Running-Back Drills

Handoffs

This drill is used to teach players the correct position of their hands, elbows when delivering and receiving the football on a handoff. The drill starts with two single lines facing each other ten yards apart. The first player in one of the lines jogs toward the first player in the opposite line. Both players stay to the left of each other. As the player from the first line jogs by the player waiting, he places the football on the stomach of the waiting player, making sure it's handed off correctly. The player waiting in the second line has his inside elbow up and his outside elbow down. When the football is placed on his stomach, he rolls his upper arm over the top and cradles it with his lower arm, carrying the ball with both arms around it. He then jogs back toward the other line, handing the ball off in the same manner to the next player in the opposite line. The players, after handing the ball off, go to the end of the line to come back the opposite way. After they have gone through the line performing handoffs to the left, they switch sides staying to the right of each other. The players need to look at the position of the football, making sure it's placed correctly. The player receiving the handoff looks straight ahead, never looking at the football. Players should use both hands to hand the football off.

Points to Remember:

1. *Don't let players go too fast.*
2. *Look at where you place the football, make sure of the handoff.*
3. *Players after receiving the handoff should jog back toward the opposite line with high knees until just before they hand the football off.*

Pitch Drill

Pitch drill starts with running backs forming a single line facing front and five yards deep behind the quarterback. The quarterback calls out the cadence (set go), and the first player in line runs the 28 sweep, taking the pitch from the quarterback. A second quarterback steps in and calls the cadence. The next player steps in and runs the sweep and receives the pitch. When the players have gone through numerous pitches for the 28 sweep, you run the opposite direction and run the 27 sweep.

Swing Pass

Swing pass is set up the same as pitch drill. Each time a new player steps in and runs a swing pattern to the right, losing ground then catching the ball and turning upfield for ten yards, then run the football back to the quarterback. After a number of swing passes to the right, you switch and throw swing passes to the left.

Points to Remember (Sweep Pitch):

1. *Pitch the football firmly and lead the back.*
2. *QB reverse steps big enough to lead and see the pitch back.*
3. *Make the players run full speed for game simulation.*

Points to Remember (Swing Pass):

1. *QB takes a five-step drop before passing the football.*
2. *Running backs lose ground on your swing pattern.*
3. *Receivers run the ball back to the QB, no walking.*

Ball Stripping

In this drill, two players will run twenty yards down the field. One player will run behind the other, holding onto the back of his jersey with one hand slowing him down while reaching around with the other hand trying to knock the football loose with his fist. At twenty yards, they switch positions and come back the other way. This is a half-speed drill.

Blocking Running Backs

Set up a player holding a blocking dummy five yards downfield. Put the other players in a single line. One player at a time from their offensive stance runs at the dummy from five yards and blocks the dummy. This is a straight man-on-man block driving the defensive man back seven counts and turning him to the right or left away from the ballcarrier. At the end of the block, the blocker takes the dummy and holds it for the next player in line. After all the players have gone through, the man-on-man block moves the blocking dummy to the right like you would be blocking a defensive end. Have your players open step to the right on the first time through and block the dummy _inside out_, attacking the dummy with their outside shoulder and turning the dummy in seven counts to the outside. This is a practice block for your 26 power. The next time though have the players block the dummy with their inside shoulder _outside in_ to practice the 28 sweep. When your players have gone through enough times, switch directions and move the dummy to the left side and run the drill again.

Offensive Receivers

One-handed catch drill starts with one line of receivers to the right and one line of receivers to the left ten yards from the quarterbacks throwing to them. Two quarterbacks are placed in the middle throwing short slant passes to the receivers, catching the ball with on hand. After a number of throws, the receivers change lines and catch with the other hand. Quarterbacks should rotate and throw the opposite direction.

Receivers' Running Patterns

Receivers stay in the same lines as one-hand catch and start running routes, making sure to switch lines after catching the football and returning it to the quarterback. Pass patterns should include slants, hooks, sideline, post, flag, and go patterns.

Quarterback Drills

One Knee

One-knee drill has the quarterbacks on one knee ten yards apart throwing the football accurately and using the correct form. After a short time, they move a few yards back and continue the warm-up.

Short Catch

Quarterbacks play catch with the football at fifteen yards and back up slowly, warming up, and end the drill with playing long catch.

Side to Side

Quarterbacks with partners spread out and move right and left with each other, passing the football back and forth as they move. When ready, they move front to back once again, passing the football back and forth.

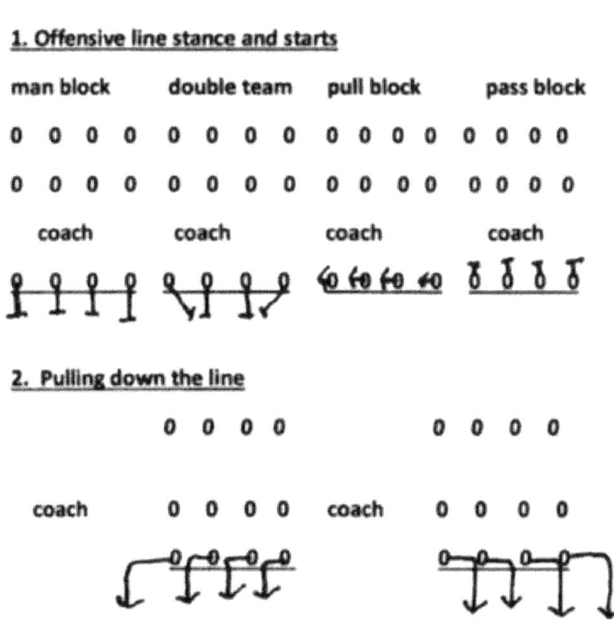

Offensive Drill Continued

4.Offensive backs (handoffs)

coach

5. Quaterback pitch and swing pass drill.

coach

Offensive Drills Continued

6. Ball stripping

X0 X0 X0 X0   X-0→

coach

X0 X0 X0 X0   X-0→

7. Offensive back blocking

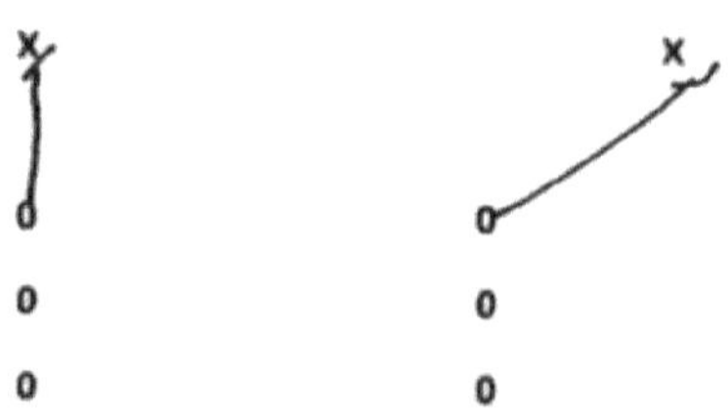

CHAPTER 8

Defense

Introduction

Earlier I talked about the 5-2 defense being our base package. It allows our players to read certain keys on running plays and passing plays. Once our defensive players have lined up correctly and the ball is hiked, they check their gap responsibility and then react to the football. The key is how fast can you carry out your assignment and react to the football. As a nose guard, I remember being quick off the ball. While I was taking on the offensive linemen, I was also finding the football and starting my pursuit. My angle of pursuit was very important to put myself in a position to make the tackle. The key was doing all of this with strength, quickness, and agility. I try to coach players that you do not want to spend a lot of time with the offensive block. When the ball is hiked, take him on, release him, and fly to the football. Do not get tied up with his block, keep the offensive blocker at arms' length so you can release and pursue. One more thing, never let the offensive linemen turn your body or drive you backward. Stay square to the line of scrimmage for as long as you can. If you're pursuing the ballcarrier to the outside, remember to always keep you outside arm free.

When you're rushing the passer, it's a different story. When you read a pass, it is an all-out gang fight trying to get to the quarterback. You attack the offensive linemen in a variety of ways. One method is the bull rush. You pin your ears back and charge the offensive linemen trying to drive him backward into the quarterback and collapse the pocket. If you have a good size and strength, this method can be effective. Another method is called the swim method. You act like your bull rushing, but on your first step, you step toward the outside of the blocker, throwing your inside arm under his outside arm while dipping down and elevating his arm then stepping past his block. If you're smaller than the offensive linemen and quicker, this method could be effective. The last rush is the spin technique. When the ball is hiked, the defensive linemen take a step toward the inside with their outside foot while making contact with the offensive linemen and then spin quickly on that same foot back to the outside, trying to get the offensive linemen off balance and getting past him. Pass rushing is not easy and it takes great determination to get to the quarterback. When rushing the passer, defensive linemen should stay in their containment lanes. We have all seen where the QB drops back for a pass on third down, and the defensive linemen lose their containment. The QB sees an opening and runs for twenty yards and another first down. STAY IN YOUR CONTAINMENT LANES!

Nose Guard

The nose guard lines head up on the center. His job is to control the center and be responsible for both A gaps on running plays. Once his gaps are checked, he flies to the football and makes the tackle. If he reads a pass, his responsibility is to check for the draw or screen pass. As the pass play develops, he watches the QB always keeping him in front waiting for the QB to try and run the football or throw a screen pass.

Linebackers

Linebackers line up and head up on the guards and five yards off the ball. If the linebackers read an inside run, they step with their inside shoulder, meeting the blocker and filling the B gaps. If the right linebacker reads an outside run to his right, he fills off the butt of the defensive end and contains the D gap or the outside while the left linebacker steps to his right and fills the right linebacker's B gap. It's just the opposite if the linebackers read an outside run to the left. The left linebacker fills off the butt of the defensive end and contains the D gap while the right linebacker slides down to his left and fills the B gap. If the linebackers read a pass, they both drop step with their outside foot and run toward the hook zone ten yards deep, reading the tight end for a dump pass or outside receivers for slant pass across the middle.

Defensive Tackle

The defensive tackles line up on the outside shoulder of the offensive tackle. The defensive tackle's job is to contain the C gap and take on the double-team block by the tight end blocking down with the offensive tackle. If the tight end releases downfield and the offensive tackle blocks down; the defensive tackle must turn to his inside and take on the pulling offensive guard. He meets the guard putting his inside shoulder on the offensive guard's chest, plugging the running lane. Defensive tackles on pass plays are responsible for outside pass rush and containment of the quarterback if he tries to run.

Defensive Ends

The defensive end's job is to never let the outside running game turn the corner. On the inside-running game, the defensive end will check outside first then close down and help contain inside. The defensive end always pursues running plays away from him, getting as deep as the deepest back and checking for reverse. On pass plays, he rushes the passer on the tight end side, checking his outside for a swing pass. He lines up on the outside shade of the tight end with inside foot forward and hands in front to protect himself from the offensive tight end trying to hook him.

Defensive Backs

There are three basic pass protection defenses. *Cover one* is a straight man-to-man coverage. The corners take the outside receivers and the strong safety covers the tight end while the free safety can roam. The linebackers drop at a forty-five-degree angle to their hook zones and slide to the flat or blitz.

Cover two is a zone defense. When flow comes toward the weakside, the corner covers the flat for the out pattern and watches for a swing pass. The free safety slides over and covers outside third to the weakside while the strong safety takes the middle. The strongside corner covers the strongside outside third. The linebackers drop at a 45-degree angle to their hook zones. If flow goes the other way, the strongside corner would cover the flat and look for the swing pass. The strongside safety would cover the outside third while the free safety covers the middle. The weakside corner would simply back up and cover his outside third.

In *cover three* the free safety and the strong safety would split half the field on the deep pass, each being responsible for half the field. The corners would cover the flat on both the weak and strong sides. The linebackers would cover the hook zones.

The cornerbacks always line up just outside the receiver five to seven yards deep. Their outside foot is forward so they can see the quarterback easier. On the snap of the football, they take three read steps backward to read a pass or run then cover their responsibility. On occasion, they move up on the receiver and shuck him at the line of scrimmage slowing him up and not letting him out free.

The free safety and strong safety line up seven to ten yards off the ball. On the snap, they take three read steps backward and read the quarterback for a pass or run. If run, they fill and help stop the run, and if pass, they cover their zone. No matter whether they're in man-to-man or zone coverage, they always play pass first then run.

Defensive Stunts and Blitzing

Stunts are a part of the defensive scheme that can confuse the defense and open pathways to the quarterback or ballcarrier. Stunts need to be done at the right time with speed and deception. I used three stunts on the defensive line to create a pathway into the offensive backfield.

Linebacker Scrap Strong

The first stunt involves the strongside linebacker and the strong defensive tackle. We scrap the strongside linebacker to the C gap off the hip of the defensive tackle. The defensive tackle slants down in front of the linebacker to the B gap. They are both simply changing gap responsibilities. We only loop to the strongside. When we run the loop, our free and strong safety help support the middle.

Tackle Loop Strong and Weak

The second stunt involves the defensive tackle and the defensive end. When we call a tackle loop strong, then our defensive end to the strongside slants down into the C gap. The defensive tackle loops outside taking the D gap and stops outside running plays and pass rushes taking the outside containment lane. The defensive tackle and defensive end are really just switching responsibilities to confuse the defense. We run tackle loop strong 95 percent of the time and tackle loop weak 5 percent.

Linebacker Way Out Strong or Weak

The third defensive stunt is called way out strong. This stunt involves the linebacker scraping way outside while the defensive end slants down into the C gap, and the defensive tackle slants down into B and the linebacker fills off the defensive end and takes the outside or the D gap. We never scrap both linebackers at the same time. Most of the time, we scrap to the strongside; it confuses the offenses' blocking assignments and free our linebacker to get to the running plays outside.

The Blitz

The blitz is a very aggressive approach to our defensive scheme. I've used the blitz with my linebackers over and over to keep the pressure on the offense. Remember with every blitz you run, there's the chance of running right past the play. It can be good and not so good; run it for a reason. I run the blitz to keep the pressure on the quarterback and to stop running or passing plays before they develop.

Linebacker Blitz

We simply signal which linebacker will blitz, and before the football is hiked, our linebacker will line up in the gap and try to explode through and sack the quarterback or hit the ballcarrier before the play develops. It's important that the defensive backs know the blitz is on so they can help cover for the blitzing linebacker. Once in a while, you have a gifted linebacker that seems to know where the football is going and really disrupts a defense by his blitzing. In this case, the blitz can be very effective.

The Safety and Corner Blitz

The safety and corner blitz is just another weapon to disrupt the offense and gain the advantage. At times, I will send one of my cornerbacks or safeties on a blitz, sacking the quarterback before he decides to run or pass the football. If I call a corner blitz, the safety nearest the corner will slide over and take the outside third of the field when the ball is hiked. The other safety will take the middle and we will have rotated correctly to cover the field for a pass or run. We can blitz any defensive back anytime by rotating.

Basic 5-2 Defense and Gaps

stronside linebacker scrape

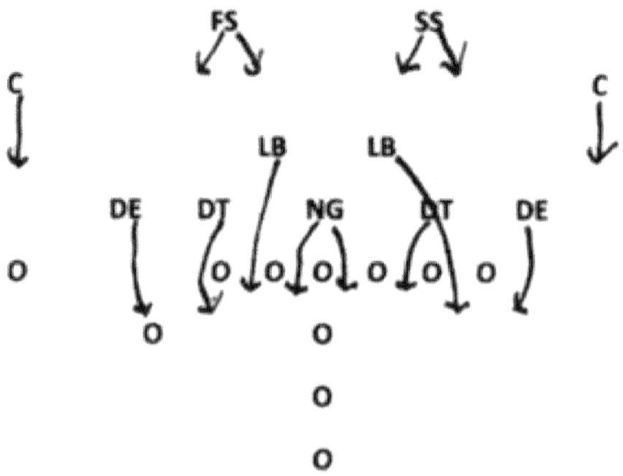

strongright linebacker scrap

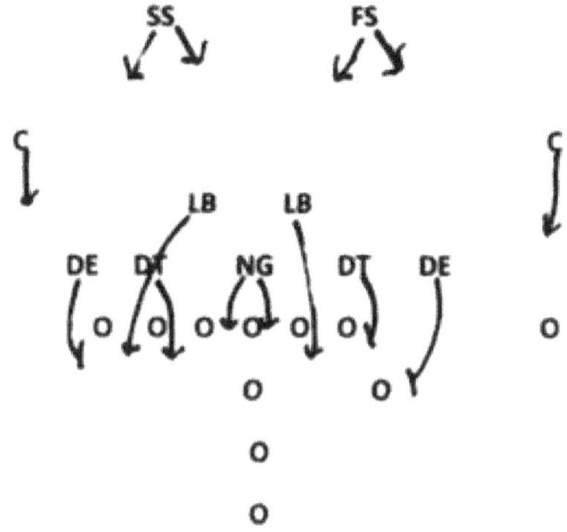

stronside tackle loop

strongside tackle loop

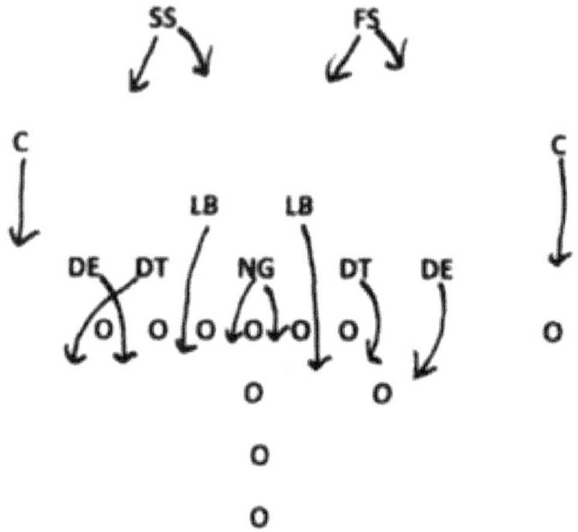

Linebacker way out strong

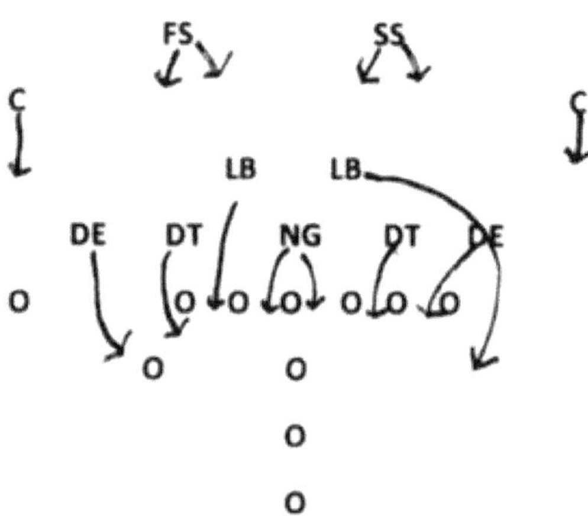

Goal Line Defense

The Gap Eight

The gap-eight defense is used inside the ten-yard line or in a short-yardage situation. The gap eight puts eight defensive players on the line of scrimmage, each having an assigned gap. When the football is hiked, all eight players fire out through their assigned gaps. They stay low getting to the heels of the offensive lineman plugging their running lane and stopping the ballcarrier. The defensive backs cheat up like linebackers to help stop the run. If it's a pass, the defensive backs will drift back and cover the middle and outside third. If the offense uses a wide receiver, the cornerback will cover him man-to-man and play him on his inside shade.

Gap Eight Responsibilities

Defensive Ends

Defensive ends line up on the outside shoulder of the tight ends. Their inside foot is forward and their hands are out in front to protect themselves from being hooked by the tight end. Their job is to rush, keeping their outside arm free and stopping the outside running game. They meet the fullback or blocker with their inside shoulder, keeping their outside arm free to be able to release and pursue the ballcarrier. If the run is inside, they close down and help contain the play as it develops. They pursue until the whistle is blown.

Defensive Tackles and Nose Guard

Defensive tackles and nose guard line up in their assigned gaps using a four-point stance. On the snap of the football, they fire through their gaps fighting to get to the heels of the offensive line plugging their gap. They stay low making sure to get under the offensive blocker's shoulder pads to stop his charge. They make the tackle or pursue it until the whistle is blown.

Linebackers

Defensive linebackers come up to the line of scrimmage and line up in their assigned gaps using a four-point stance. On the snap of the football, they fire through their gaps fighting to get to the heels of the offensive line plugging their gap. They stay low, making sure to get under the offensive blocker's shoulder pads to stop his charge. They make the tackle or pursue it until the whistle is blown.

Defensive Backs

Defensive backs line up five to seven yards deep behind the defensive line to help stop the run. If the offensive team lines up with a wide receiver, the cornerback on that side will take him man-to-man. The corner will line on to the receiver's inside, taking away the quick slant pass. The defensive backs pursue to the tackle or until the whistle is blown.

CHAPTER 9

Defensive Drills

Tackling Drills

Form Tackling

This drill is form tackling only. Form two lines five yards apart with players facing each other; one line is the tackler the other line is the ballcarrier. The tackler takes his first step with his right foot then left foot and plants his right foot while lowering his butt and coming up through the ballcarrier's chest, wrapping his arms around then lifts and carries him five yards downfield.

Points to Remember:

1. *This is form tackling only.*
2. *On contact, a player should be lowering his hips and coming up through the ballcarrier wrapping their arms and lifting.*
3. *Tacklers should keep their camera (butt) facing downfield.*
4. *The tackler should always have his eyes up for safety.*

Angle Tackling

This drill is half speed only until the players demonstrate a good understanding of the drill. Form two lines with players facing one behind the other seven yards apart. One line will be the tacklers and the other line will be the ballcarriers. The coach stands ten yards in front and in the middle of the two lines. On the coach's command, the first tackler and the first ballcarrier run at a forty-five-degree angle toward the coach. The tackler meets the ballcarrier by lowering his butt, coming up through his chest and wrapping his arms as he lifts and drives him five yards downfield. He keeps his head and eyes up at all times, squaring his camera (butt) downfield (see diagram below).

Points to Remember:

1. *Until the players understand the drill, this drill is half speed only.*
2. *Make players run at a forty-five-degree angle toward the coach, don't let them avoid each other.*
3. *This is a five-count tackle, driving the ballcarrier up the field after contact.*
4. *Make sure the tacklers' eyes are up. When tackling, players should always have their eyes up looking at the ballcarrier, never down at the ground. Looking down can cause them to miss the tackle.*

Open-Field Tackling

Place two blocking bags ten yards apart. Form two lines of players, sending one line of players to each blocking bag and line up outside the bags. Place your first player from each line facing each other in the center between the bags and back them up ten yards. Explain to them that you will throw a football to one of them. The one that gets the football is the ballcarrier and the other is the tackler. The ballcarrier after catching the football must stay between the blocking bags and run past the tackler, trying to score without getting tackled and staying between the bags. This is a three-quarter speed drill until the players understand what to do. For safety, players should be no more than ten yards apart.

Points to Remember:

1. *Keep players back from the drill for safety so they don't get kicked while watching.*
2. *The tackler and ballcarrier should be no more than ten yards apart.*
3. *Have a quick whistle to end the tackle.*
4. *Explain to your tacklers they must get under control to make a good tackle.*
5. *The ballcarrier should try to make moves to trick the tackler.*

Sideline Tackling

Form two lines, one line will be ballcarriers on the forty-yard line at the side of the field. The other line who are tacklers will be twenty-five yards in on the field at the opposite forty-yard hash mark. One ballcarrier at a time will run down the sideline while the tackler pursues him at the correct angle and either knocks him out of bounds or make the tackle if he tries to cut back. The purpose of this drill is for the tacklers to get under control, always keeping the ballcarrier on their outside shoulder so he can't run past the tackler if he makes a cut.

Points to Remember

1. *The tackler needs to be under control.*
2. *Be ready for the cutback.*
3. *Always keep the ballcarrier on your outside shoulder so he can't cut back.*

Defensive Lineman

Stance and Starts

Form four lines on the goal line. From your stance fire out five yards, go around, and get in line. The coach is checking your stance and starts.

Watch the Football

Form four lines on the goal line. The coach places the football on the line of scrimmage in the middle of the four lines and calls out snap counts trying to get the defensive players to jump offsides. When the coach moves the football, the players fire out five yards, go around, and go to the end of their lines. This drill teaches the players to watch the ball and not get pulled offsides by the QB's voice.

Points to Remember:

1. *Have a good stance, don't jump offside, and watch the ball.*
2. *Hustle back in line to go again.*
3. *The coach uses a variety of snap counts to try and get players to jump. Be loud and vary your voice.*

Shoulder on the Chest (on One Knee)

All football drills are half speed until the players demonstrate they understand the drill. Form two lines with players facing each other standing one yard apart. One line is the offense and the other line is the defense. Offense players take a three-point stance in front of the defensive player. The defensive players are facing the offensive players and kneeling down with one knee on the ground and one knee up. When the coach says go, the offensive players come forward one or two steps to block the defensive players. The defensive players place their right shoulder pad on the chest of the offensive player as they lift them up, using their back, forearms, and lower legs to neutralize their charge.

Points to Remember:

1. *This is a form drill and is one or two steps forward by the offensive player.*
2. *The purpose of this drill is to get under the offensive man's block and put your shoulder pad on his chest while lifting with your back, forearms, and legs to raise him up and neutralize his charge.*
3. *The drill will start out ugly. When it looks good, the players will know how to use the strongest part of their body to stop an offensive block.*

Shoulder on the Chest, Square Him Up, and Release

This drill is shoulder on the chest, squaring the offensive blocker up then getting him away so you can release and go tackle the ballcarrier. Use the same formation as the shoulder on the chest drill. Everything is the same except this time your players are going to square the offensive blocker up and get rid of him. The defensive player puts his shoulder pad on the chest while bringing his forearm forward and up through the blocker and getting him in front at arms' length and then getting rid of him and going to the football.

Points to Remember:

1. *Shoulder on the chest, squaring the blocker up and flying to the football are all done at light speed in one movement.*
2. *You cannot get driven back or turn to one side by the offensive blocker.*
3. *Get to the football and make the tackle.*

Double Team and Trap

The double team and trap drills are to help the defensive lineman read the offensive blockers. The offensive blockers are going to do one of four blocks. The first will be a man block which is simply the offensive blocker coming straight at you trying to block you downfield or turn you in a certain direction. In this case, you would use your shoulder on the chest, squaring him up and not giving any ground then releasing and flying to the football. The second block could be the double-team block where the tight end would block down on you with the defensive tackle using the double-team block, pushing you out of the running lane. To stop the double-team block, a defensive lineman must read it very quickly. When he sees the double team, he simply drops down low under the blockers and starts crawling to the heels of the offensive lineman. It's important that he gets underneath the double team. If he stands up, the tight end and the defensive tackle will have a serious advantage in taking him out of the play. Staying underneath their block and plugging the running lane have a much better outcome. The third block is the trap block. In this situation, the offensive tight end and offensive tackle blow right by the defensive tackle, leaving him untouched. When this happens, the defensive tackle needs to immediately read this and turn to the inside. The backside-offensive guard will be pulling down the line of scrimmage to trap him, hoping he won't be looking. The defensive tackle needs to turn inside and meet the pulling guard with his inside shoulder on the chest and squaring him up to the line of scrimmage and plugging up the running lane. Normally if the backside guard is pulling, the ballcarrier is right behind him. The fourth and final block is the pass block. If they show pass blocking, we pass rush, keeping the quarterback in front of us and not losing containment.

The Four Reads

1. *It could be a straight man block by the offensive tackle.*
2. *They might double team down, trying to push the defensive tackle out of the play.*
3. *If there's no double team or man block by the offensive tackle, it could be a trap, and the backside offensive guard is coming down the line.*
4. *The last possible read in this drill would be they all three show pass block.*

Points to Remember:

1. *Go under the double team.*
2. *Meet the pulling guard with the inside shoulder on the chest and lift then square him up to the line of scrimmage to plug the running lane.*
3. *The ballcarrier will be following the pulling guard on the trap.*
4. *When it's a straight-man block, use a shoulder on the chest, square him up, and release to the football.*

Pass Rush (Bull, Swim, and Spin Rush)

Pass-rush drill is simply that. We line up four offensive linemen and four defensive linemen facing each other on the line of scrimmage with correct splits. The coach stands behind the offensive players like a quarterback and calls the cadence. When the ball is hiked, we first practice the bull rush always staying in our containment lanes and not letting the quarterback escape. Then we will move on to the swim move and then finally the spin move. The drill is full speed and players work hard to get to the QB. We use our own defensive players for offensive pass blockers during this drill and rotate players at the end of every play.

Points to Remember:

1. *Be relentless to get to the football.*
2. *Be deceptive on your pass-rush techniques.*
3. *Stay in your containment lane; keep the quarterback in front of you.*

Team-Pursuit Drill

We practice pursuit drill in our defensive team period, or sometimes we use it for conditioning. Team-pursuit drills need to be high energy and push the players to be quicker to the football. Getting a large number of tacklers to the football is important and produces good defense. In this drill the entire defense lines up in their defensive positions on the ball. The coach will stand on the offensive side of the football with a running back five yards deep to his right and a second running back five yards deep to his left. When the coach tosses the football to one of the running backs, he immediately takes off and runs around his end toward the sidelines, and the defensive players pursue him. All the defensive players must touch the ballcarrier before they can stop running. Once they have touched the ballcarrier, they jog back around the drill and get ready for their next turn. On the coach's signal, another group runs out, lines up, and the coach starts the drill once again.

Points to Remember:

1. *Slow pursuit loses football games.*
2. *Demand speed and teamwork.*
3. *Your ballcarriers need to be fast.*

Drive Drill

We use the drive drill to find out who are football players. This drill tells us who wants to play and who likes to tackle. This is one of our most spirited drills and can set the tone for competition very quickly. In this drill, the offense will have two offensive linemen and an offensive center to hike the football. They will line up on the line of scrimmage with a quarterback behind the center calling the snap count. Two running backs will line up five yards deep behind the offensive guards. On the snap of the football, both the running backs will dive straight ahead over the guards. The quarterback will turn and hand the football off to either back who will try and score. On the other side of the football will be two defensive linemen lined up over the offensive guards and one linebacker five yards deep over the center. When the ball is hiked, the defense keeps the offense from scoring. There are two blocking bags ten yards apart on the line of scrimmage. The players must stay within these bags for the score to count. The players watching will cheer on the other players.

Points to Remember:

1. *This needs to be competitive and spirited.*
2. *Tell the players you want to see who wants to play football.*
3. *This drill is full speed and not a drill to be used every day.*

Defensive Linebackers

Stance and Starts

This drill will warm up linebackers while checking their movement. Put your linebackers on the side of the football field in two lines facing the field five yards apart. Using the marked lines on the football field, tell the first player in each line to take a position five yards on the field facing the coach in their defensive stance. The coach will point the tip of the football in the direction he wants the players to shuffle right, left, backward, and forward without crossing their feet and staying square to the coach. When he holds the ball over his head, they rush the coach as if it were a pass with their hands up. If the coach points the ball down, they drop to the ground on their stomach and immediately get back up running in place, ready to continue. At the end of the drill, they go to the end of the opposite line and wait for their next turn.

Points to Remember:

1. *Good stance.*
2. *Keep your eyes up and on the quarterback (coach).*
3. *Don't ever cross your feet.*
4. *Be quick!*

Shucker Drill

This drill teaches linebackers to shuck the oncoming blocker by taking him on with the inside shoulder and keeping the outside arm free to make the tackle. Just before the offensive blocker throws his block, the linebacker (shucker) lowers his inside shoulder getting under the offensive blocker's shoulder pads and coming up through his block, lifting and pushing him off to the side. To run this drill, the coach puts the players in a single line one behind the other facing forward. The first player in line steps out and turns around then backs up five yards, facing the other players to become the shucker. The coach calls out which shoulder the shucker will use to take on the blocker. On the coach's command, the first player in line runs at the shucker and tries to block him. The shucker takes him on, putting his shoulder on the blocker's chest and shucking him to the side. When the whistle blows again, the next blocker runs and tries to block the shucker and then the next player and so on. After three or four players have tried to block the shucker, he goes to the end of the line and the next player in line becomes the new shucker. The drill goes until everyone has been a shucker. Coach, remember players need to practice shucking with both shoulders.

Points to Remember:

1. *Meet the blocker with a shoulder on the chest.*
2. *The lowest shoulder pad wins.*
3. *Use your legs and back to come up through the offensive lineman's block.*
4. *Shuck him to the side so you can find the football.*

Linebacker Read Drill

This is a linebacker drill to read dive, sweep, pass, and the quarterback keeping the ball and trying to run. It's asking the linebackers to react to the quarterback's movement. The drill starts with two lines of players facing the coach five yards apart, one behind and the other waiting their turn. The first player in front of each line steps out five yards, turns, and faces the coach, getting in a linebacker stance. The coach takes a quarterback stance facing the linebackers. On the snap of the ball, he turns right or left, putting the ball out like he is going to hand off on a dive. The linebackers run toward the coach calling the dive. If the coach tucks the ball and runs down the line of scrimmage to the outside, the players pursue down the line to stop the outside run. If the coach drops straight back like he is going to pass, then the linebackers call out a pass as they fly to the hook zones or pass responsibility. Finally if the coach drops straight back and acts like he is going to pass, the linebackers start their pass responsibility until they see the coach bring the ball down, tuck it, and start to run. They react and converge on him under control.

Points to Remember:

1. *This is a reaction drill to read the play. Players must react at lightning speed.*
2. *Linebackers should be taking a read step forward, always looking for the run first then pass.*
3. *Use the lines on the football field to line up players for the drill.*

Defensive Backs

Stance and Starts

This drill is done from the sidelines using the lines on the field to help the players track their direction. The drill starts with one line of players facing the field. The first player steps out and takes a good defensive stance on the line. When the coach lifts the football, he starts to backpedal. The next player steps out and gets ready for the coach to lift the ball a second time, and the second player starts his backpedal while the first player watching the coach lift the ball a second time plants his outside foot and runs at a forty-five-degree angle back toward the sideline to play run. On the third lift of the ball by the coach, the first player drop steps with his outside foot at a forty-five-degree angle toward the hook zone, yelling pass. On the fourth lift from the coach, the first player stops, plants his outside foot, and runs a straight line back to the sideline and starts a new line to run the drill back the other way once all the players have finished their progressions. When every player has gone through, the coach will run the drill the opposite direction back the other way.

Shadow Drill

The shadow drill is a practice playing man-to-man coverage and staying with the receiver who is making different moves down the field. The defensive player practices the correct footwork to stay with him. The coach puts the defensive backs in two separate lines twenty yards apart, facing down the field. The first player in both lines steps out to play pass defense. The next player in line becomes the offensive receiver. When the coach says go, the offensive players run at half speed down the field, making different cuts while the defensive player backpedals, staying with the receivers, cuts and drop steps with their correct foot toward the cut. When the players get twenty yards downfield, they stop and switch positions and perform the drill coming back the other way. When they return, they go to the end of the line and the next two players go.

Points to Remember:

1. *Make sure the receiver is making a good cut and going five yards then make the next cut.*
2. *The defensive back should have his butt down and his nose over his toes.*
3. *Once they understand the drill, speed it up.*

Defensive Drills

1. Form Tackling

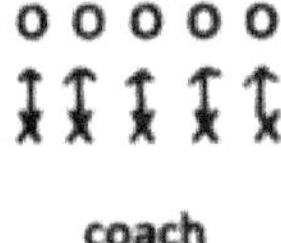

coach

2. Angle tackling

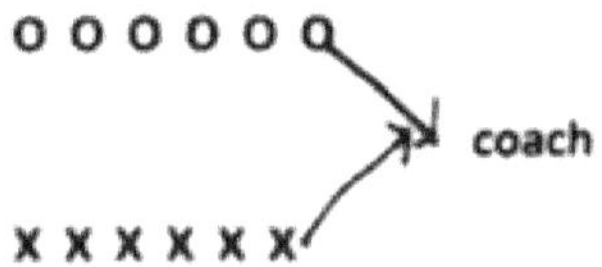

Defensive Drills Continued

3. Open field tackling

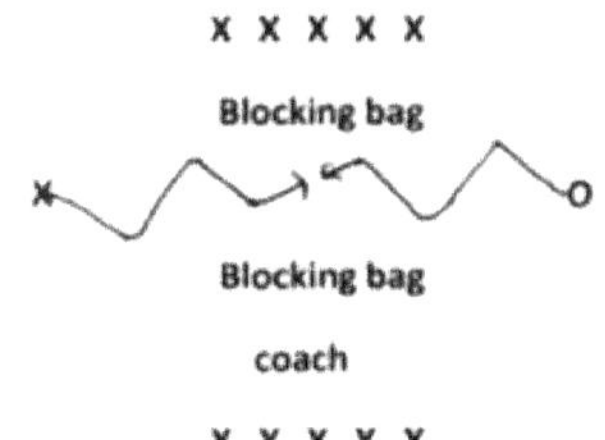

4. Sideline tackling

Defensive Drills Continued

5. Defensive Stance and Starts

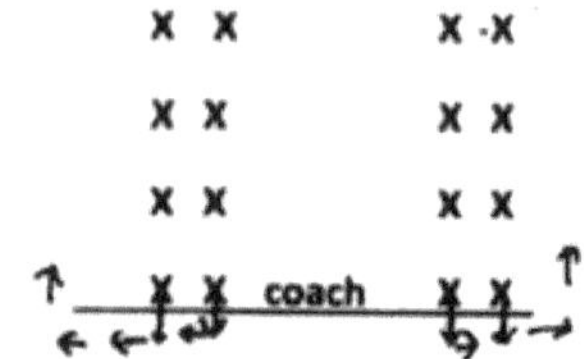

6. Watch the Football (don't go off sides)

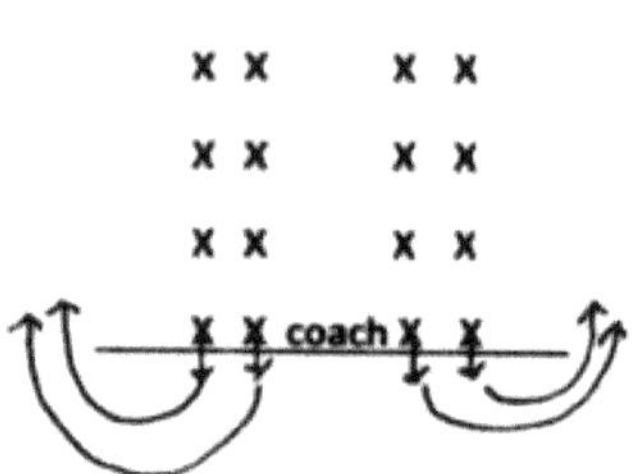

Defensive Drills Continued

7. Shoulder on the Chest

Coach

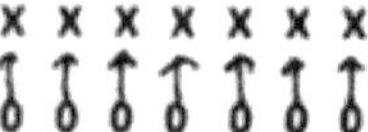

8. Shoulder on the chest square him up

Coach

Defensive Drills Continued

9. Double team and trap Drill

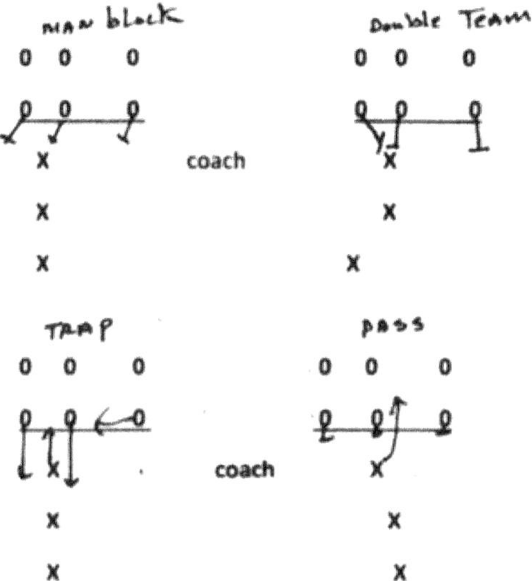

Defensive Drills Continued

11. Pass Rush (bull,swim and spin rush)

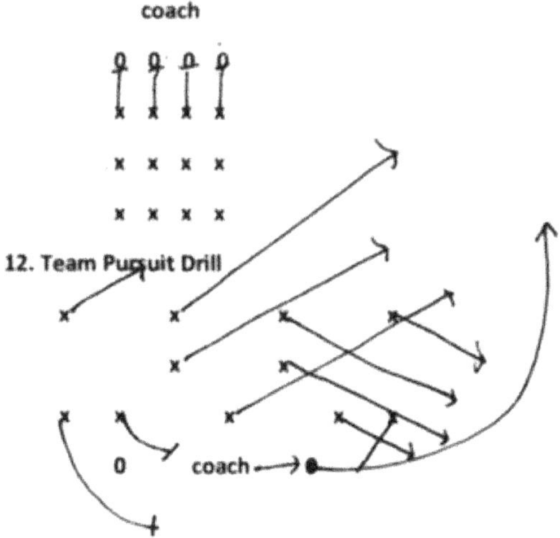

12. Team Pursuit Drill

Defensive Drills Continued

10. Drive Drill

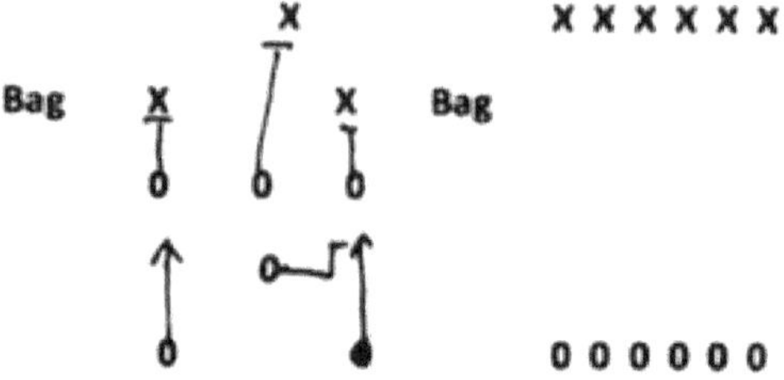

11. Defensive Linebacker (stance and Starts)

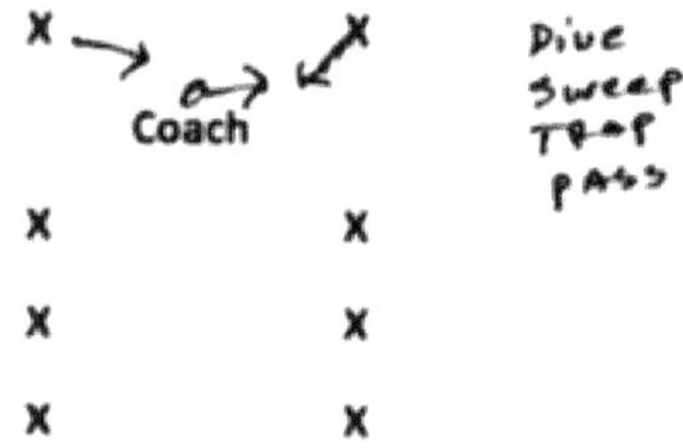

Defensive Drills Continued

12. Shucker Drill

13. Linebacker Read Drill

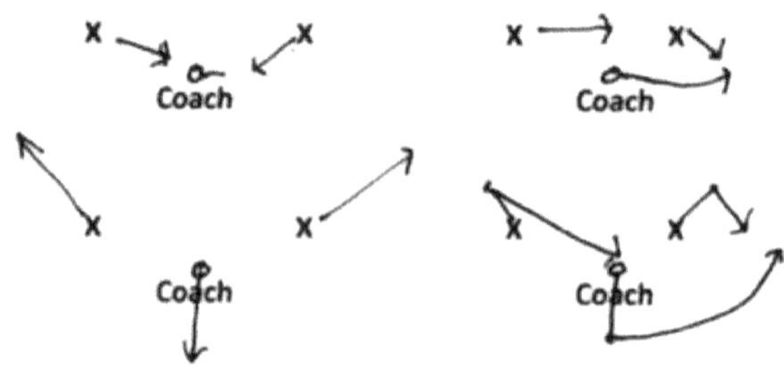

Defensive Drills Continued

14. Defensive Backs stance and starts

Coach

X X X X X X X

!5. Defensive back shadow drill

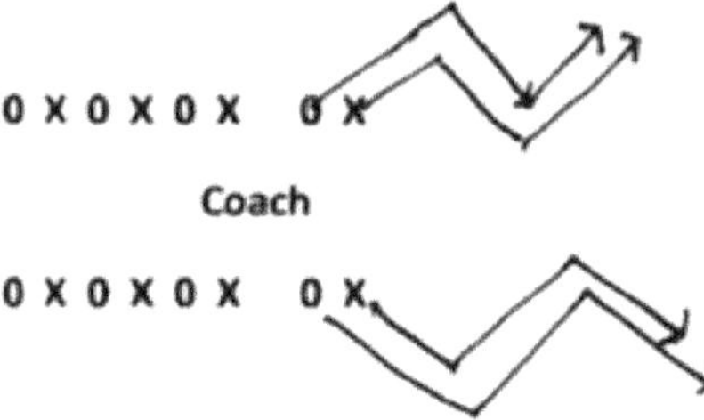

Coach

0 X 0 X 0 X   0 X

CHAPTER 10
Special Teams

Punt Team

We all want our football teams to be good at special teams, but finding the practice time is not always easy. Just the same, it needs to be a serious part of your football program. A good punter supported by a great punt-coverage team can drive the other team down the field and put them at a big disadvantage. Good punters will spend many hours of their own time to become effective and consistent in kicking the football. When your team punts during a football game, it will be important for the center to deliver a consistent snap thirteen to fifteen yards, so the punter has at least three seconds to punt the football untouched. After the punter punts the football, it's his job to yell the direction of the punt to the coverage team, for example right, left, short, long. Once the center has snapped the football to the punter, the offensive line must be ready to hold up the defensive rush for two seconds then release and get downfield to cover the punt. When covering the punt coverage, players run downfield in their assigned lanes avoiding blockers and converging on the ballcarrier. When they are five yards from the ballcarrier, they get under control, squaring their shoulders to make a sure tackle. All coverage players should be ready for the punt returner to make a bad catch or fumble the football.

When deciding on your punter, I've found good punters have a natural ability and leg strength to kick the football. Coaches need to spend time coaching potential punters about using the correct form, for example how to hold the ball in their hands, the correct angle to drop the football, and where the football contacts the instep of your foot. With many hours of continuous practice, a punter will start to develop, feel, and understand the techniques needed to be a consistent punter. As a young boy, I learned to punt the football out in the street in front of my house. To get a good height, I would try and punt the football over the telephone wires that ran across the street. Those days are gone now, most punters go down to their high school field with a friend or parent to practice. Part of becoming a good punter depends on the dedication shown by the player.

Punt Return

Good clean catches on punt returns are important and at times very challenging if the weather is bad and the wind is blowing or the football is wet. Sometimes it's just better to stay away from a punted football. A badly punted football can accidentally hit the ground and take a wild bounce, touching one of the punt-return players. The ball then becomes live and can be recovered by the punt team for possession and an automatic first down. In good conditions, catching a well-punted football can mean positive yardage by the ballcarrier, advancing it up the field. The punt returner also has the option of putting his hand straight up in the air, waving it back and forth to signal a fair catch which allows him to catch the football untouched. The football will then be spotted where the catch occurred. When picking a player to return punts, I always looked for someone mature, elusive, confident, and having good hands. It's a good idea your punt returners practice catching badly punted footballs as well as the good ones to learn which punts are returnable and which punts you should leave alone.

When the football is punted, the return team can rush the punter and try to block the punt or delay the punt team to give their punt returner time to catch the football and run. With good teamwork, some teams will hold the punt team up then release them downfield and set up a wall close to the sideline, giving the punt returner a return lane to run. Younger players might not have time to set up a punt return if their punts aren't long enough. In this case, I would coach players to slow their guy up and block him to the right or left without holding.

Kickoffs

Kickoffs start a football game. Whichever team wins the coin flip before the game starts has the option to receive or kick off to the other team. The team losing the coin flip will have the option of choosing which goal they want to defend. A team that receives the kickoff at the start of the game will automatically kickoff to the other team at the start of the second half. Other kickoffs take place when a team has scored a touchdown or field goal. The kickoff is a starting point for the receiving team to catch the football and run it back as far as they can. From that point, they will use their offensive plays to advance the ball down the field to try and score a touchdown. The kickoff team normally lines up on its forty-yard line and cannot cross the forty until the football is kicked. Once the football travels ten yards, it is a live football and either team can recover it. If the ball goes out of bounds before it travels ten yards, then it's a five-yard penalty, and the kicking team must rekick from the thirty-five-yard line. In most cases, teams will place the football in the middle of the forty-yard line when teams line up to kickoff, but it can be placed anywhere on the forty before play starts. Remember the ball only needs to travel ten yards, and it becomes a live football. Different types of kickoff can include the onside, line drive, or long kickoff. Before the kicker kicks the football, it's a good idea for him to count his players before raising his hand to signal to the referee that his team is ready to play.

When the football is kicked off, players (tacklers) will run down the field to stop the return. Tacklers need to stay in their pursuit lanes going down the field, avoiding the blockers, and closing in on the ballcarrier. Five yards from the ballcarrier, they should get under control and make a sure tackle. Tacklers should also be ready for a fumble or a loose football. The kicker is always the last man down the field in case the kickoff returner breaks through. I look for players on the kickoff team to be fast and able to avoid the blockers going down the field. It's important these players are sure tacklers and have a burning desire and the speed to stop the kickoff returner inside the twenty-yard line or thirty depending on the age group you're coaching. I always kick off to what looks like the slowest return man. If their returner is a big threat, I might tell my kicker to line drive it down the field and make the football take some weird bounces. When the kickoff team practices kickoffs, it should be full speed downfield to the ballcarrier but no tackling. Blocking should be position blocking only to eliminate needless injuries.

Kickoff Returns

Kickoff returns can be pretty exciting when you have a return man that is not only fast but has great agility and can hang on to the football. My rule is for the kickoff-return ballcarriers to hang back and move forward to catch the ball on the run then look for a seam and turn on the speed. I never really like returners who dance around trying to create their own luck, and I hate it when they run backward. Having said that, I have seen some great returns and great returners starting one direction and then stopping and going another. My rule is to catch the football on the run and pop a seam at full speed. The players blocking for the ballcarrier need to block their man as long as they can give the ballcarrier a chance to find a path toward the end zone. Once in a while. it happens; the ballcarrier goes all the way for a touchdown to the cheers from the stands. Every week the kickoff returns need to be practiced at full speed with position blocking only to stop unwanted injuries.

Extra Points

After witnessing extra points over the years, I've grown to realize their importance. Extra points occur after a touchdown has been scored. The team scoring the touchdown has the option of kicking the football off the ground from the five-yard line for one point or trying to run one offensive play from the five-yard line to score two points. You should choose which option depending on the age group of your players and your kicker's ability to kick extra points.

When lining up for kicking the extra point, the offensive line will take a two-point stance at the line of scrimmage with their hands on their knees and their right foot slightly back for better balance. The offensive linemen's splits are very small to keep the defensive team from penetrating. When the football is snapped, the line stays low and takes a balance step forward, bringing their hands up to a blocking position and neutralize the defensive charge. The extra point must be kicked quickly without problems. The football needs to be snapped to the holder correctly, and the kicker kicking the football needs to kick the football with good direction and timing. I always use my quarterbacks to be holders for kicking extra points. If a problem occurs during the extra point, the holder yells fire, fire, and the kick is abandoned. The receivers automatically release to the end zone, looking for the holder to run or pass the football.

Field Goals

Field goals are attempted by the offensive team when they have not gained enough yardage for a first down. Instead of punting the football, the offensive team feels they are close enough to try and kick the football through the upright for three points. The field-goal team sets up just like the extra point and is performed in the same manner. If the field goal is missed, the defensive becomes the offensive and is given a first down from the previous line of scrimmage. If the field goal is blocked, the football becomes live and either team can advance and is awarded a first down.

PUNT TEAM

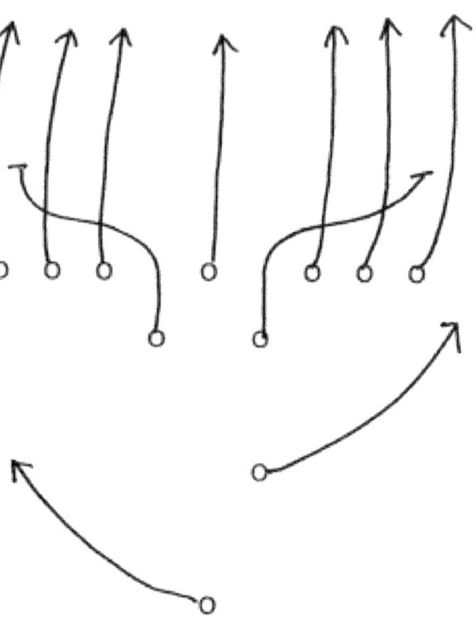

PUNT RETURN RIGHT

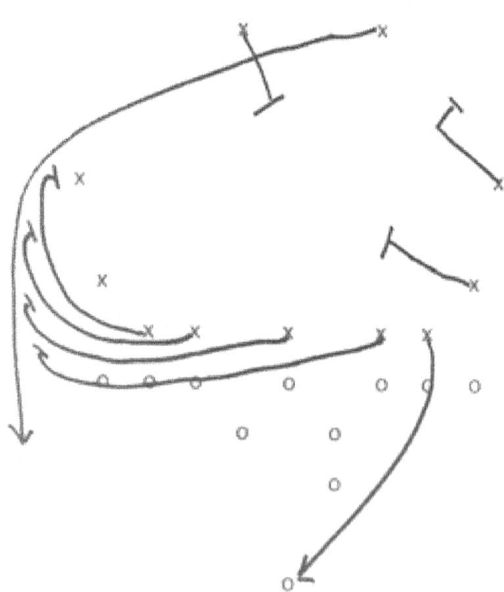

KICKOFF

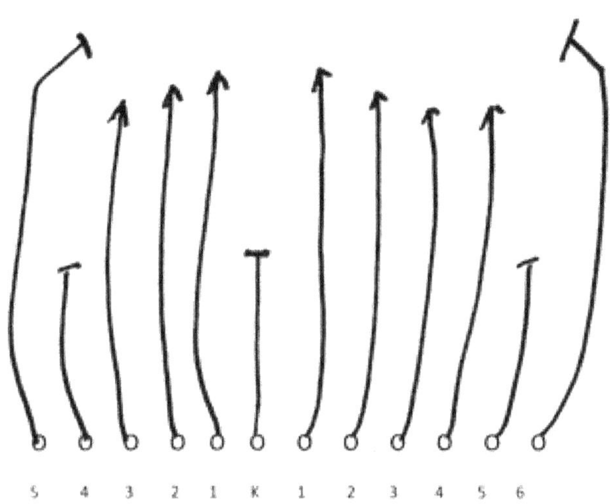

KICKOFF RETURN

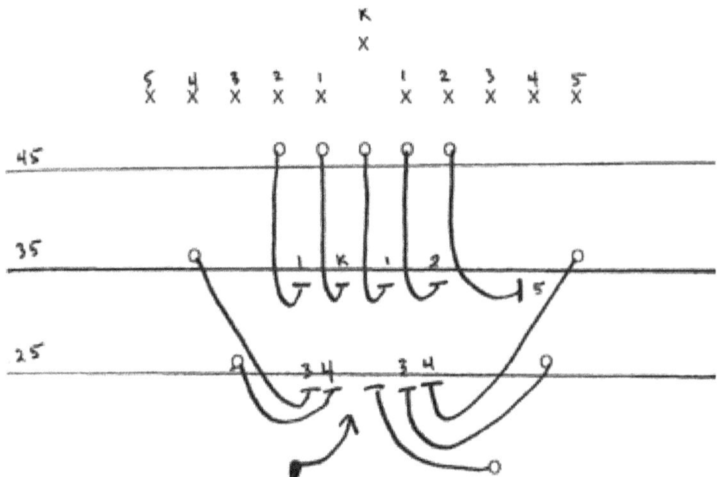

ACKNOWLEDGEMENTS

I want to thank all my fellow coaches who were a part of my football coaching and playing experiences throughout my life. I would also like to pay tribute to the hundreds of young athletes who have played or have been a part of my football programs over the years.

To my Grandsons Landon and Logan Sherman, thank you for making your grandfather so very proud. Landon I think you are a great football player and I am so proud of your efforts on the field. This book is dedicated to you and your great desire and hard work. Logan, I am just as proud of you for your ability to bring people together and lift them up.

I would like to thank Steve and Lisa Oliver for their great friendship and support over the years. Andrew and Ryan Oliver, I believe in you boys and I know you are going to make us all proud.

To my son in-law Mark, thank you for the many conversations we have had over the years about football and for being such a good husband to my daughter. To my daughters Kristyn and Heather, you are the love of my life. I know you both will remember all the shortcuts Dad took to get to the games on time.

Lastly, thank you to my wonderful wife Christi who listens to all my answers to life's problems using examples from coaching philosophies.